IN GOD'S GRIP

IN GOD'S GRIP

A JOURNEY OF HOPE

Patti Robinson

XULON PRESS

Xulon Press
2301 Lucien Way #415
Maitland, FL 32751
407.339.4217
www.xulonpress.com

Paperback ISBN-13: 978-1-6305-0489-2
Ebook ISBN-13: 978-1-6305-0490-8

TABLE OF CONTENTS

Dedication vii

Acknowledgements ix

Introduction xiii

CHAPTER 1
My Early Years. 1

CHAPTER 2
The Shattered Years 13

CHAPTER 3
Security Lost 29

CHAPTER 4
A New and Different Kind of Normal 35

CHAPTER 5
My Introduction to Christ .57

CHAPTER 6
The Diabetes Diagnosis 65

CHAPTER 7
We're Moving?. 75

CHAPTER 8
The Blind Date that Would Change My Life 87

CHAPTER 9
Considering Adoption AND Reunification 129

CHAPTER 10
A Restored Relationship 141

CHAPTER 11
The Most Priceless Gift 157

CHAPTER 12
Cancer Strikes Again 179

CHAPTER 13
Dark Memories Exposed to The Light 199

CHAPTER 14
Honoring Uncle Joe 205

CHAPTER 15
God Is Our Provider 213

CHAPTER 16
Raising Teenagers and Another Diagnosis 221

CHAPTER 17
Choosing Joy 279

DEDICATION

This book is dedicated to everyone who has either had a voice but felt like they could never use it, or who have had a voice but were afraid to use it.

And to every person who ever felt like they never mattered or that they can't seem to live above the circumstances that they find themselves living in, this is for you.

ACKNOWLEDGEMENTS

First and foremost, I would like to thank **God** for walking with me on the journey of my life and forever holding me ever so closely in His grip.

I thank my husband **Tim**, the absolute love of my life for encouraging me and motivating me to get out of my comfort zone. Thank you for always believing in me and rooting me on. So many times I was ready to give up, but you prayed me through. Your patience throughout the process of writing **In God's Grip**, *A Journey of Hope* helped me so much. It is because of you that I was able to see the writing process through. I love you bigger than big and wider than wide!

I would like to thank **Nathaniel** and **Allison** for fulfilling my hopes of motherhood. Thank you both for keeping me on my toes. I will always believe in you, love you (up to heaven and back) and pray for you.

Aunt **Tina Helder**, thank you for being such a positive role model in my life. I continue to learn from you every day. You challenge me to be real with how I feel and it has proven to be essential in my walk with Christ, knowing that He knows how I am feeling anyway. Being real with Him has allowed me to be real with myself.

Don Stubblefield, my precious bigger than me little brother, we have been through so much together and apart. I am so very proud of the man that you are and that you were able and are able to rise above life's circumstances. I honor you for the years that you put into the U.S. Air Force and I want you to know that I love you and you matter so much to me!

Aunt **Linda** and Uncle **Joe**, thank you both for taking Don and I in and raising us along with your four kids. Your unselfish act and courage in doing this allowed us to have a chance to actually be able to make choices for ourselves. I miss you. Save a place for me!

Barbara LaFarge, thank you so much for walking me through the first stage of the editing process of *In God's Grip, A Journey of Hope.*

Linda Brownell, thank you for all of the endless hours that went into reviewing and for pouring yourself into the final editing of *In God's Grip, A Journey of Hope.*

Lisa Ivey, thank you for taking what was on my heart and painting the beautiful cover of *In God's Grip, A Journey of Hope*. It truly captures the essence of that little girl who was held in the mighty grip of God.

Ezra Ivey, thank you for condensing the book cover photo and placing the perfect font into the format that worked for *In God's Grip, A Journey of Hope.*

Adam MIller, thank you ever so much for following God's lead when it came to teaching the *Theoddysey* class. It was grueling to navigate-through, but so worth the effort. I am so thankful for the tools that I learned and that this class enabled me to believe in my head and in my heart that I am a beloved child of God.

Ceres Christian Church, thank you for praying me through my battles as God turned those battles into blessings. Thank you for teaching the truth of Christ. If Ceres Christian Church ceased to exist, I know that many lives would be affected, especially mine.

Tamara Davis, thank you for investing the time and dedication in doing the last editing of *In God's Grip, A Journey of Hope* and for giving me true to your heart constructive criticism.

Xulon Publishing, you are a great team and have helped me so much through the writing process. **Alexandria Zaldivar**, thank you for believing in me and for being ever so patient with me during the entire process of writing **In God's Grip**, *A Journey of Hope.*

INTRODUCTION

Once upon a time ago this little girl lived in a very dark world with absolutely no hope. She was a victim of molestation, emotional abuse, physical abuse and she was bound by the enemy. The enemy really tried to dig his claws into this little girl's frail body. She was told that she would be nothing, do nothing, accomplish nothing and amount to nothing. She was told that she would always be alone. At 8 years old she was stripped of any comfort that she ever had when her mom died. By God's amazing and saving grace and through a miracle, He found this little girl and He enabled this little girl to not use the abuse she suffered as an excuse to throw her life away with alcohol, drugs and unhealthy relationships, but to throw the enemy the darts of "I can do all things through Christ, who strengthens me" (Philippians 4:13 NKJV) power.

God changed the life of this little girl, as He held her closely In His Grip.

Chapter 1

MY EARLY YEARS

I was born on November 20, 1967 at 10:47 am at Eden Hospital located in Castro Valley, California. My birth generated headlines in the local newspaper. "It is quite possible", the newspaper said the next day, "that the little baby girl, weighing in at 6 pounds 4 ounces, and 19 1/2 inches long is the 200,000,000th American." By that, the paper meant that the person who cracked the 200 million barrier in the U.S. population was born near that time. President Lyndon Johnson made a big deal about the milestone when he addressed a crowd in the U.S. Commerce Department lobby with a *census clock* as his backdrop. The Census Bureau had estimated the 200 millionth American likely would have been born between 10:58 am and 11:02 am that day, and their meter turned over during his speech. Life Magazine, however, decided that Robert Ken Woo Jr. of Atlanta was the 200 millionth American. He was born at 11:03 am that day. "According to the Bureau of Vital Statistics, the 200,000,000th American would have been born at approximately 11 am yesterday", the November 21, 1967 story stated, "and a check of hospitals throughout the area showed Miss Casey to be nearest to the hour." Whether it was Robert Ken Woo Jr or myself, the people of Castro Valley showered me with gifts in the event that I really was *that* child. I was given a high chair, a rocking chair, crib, toys, clothes and blankets–absolutely everything a baby girl would need. However, what they couldn't give me was the stable life that every child deserves.

Being so young, my memories are few of my mom, Judy and my father, Jim's marriage. I remember my mom often becoming frustrated with my dad when she would find candy wrappers hidden between the cushions of our couch or when he would grab her from behind and kiss her. What I was later told by my family was that my dad loved my mom, but my mom cared about my dad more like a brother than a husband. My mom had a very abusive biological dad, so when my parents met, it provided a way for my mom to escape the abuse that she had been living with.

My mom and dad divorced when I was two years old. My father moved back to where he was raised, Elmira, New York. He had always been very close to his mom and that is where she lived, so that is where he went. He did not stay in contact with me. My mom then began a relationship with a man named Bob. During the three years that my mom was with Bob, he sexually abused me. I remember being filled with such fear as I went to bed during those years. He would come into my room in the middle of the night, shake me awake (I would often only be pretending to be asleep) and carry me to a large closet room. It was here that he would take my innocence away. As he stripped me and groped me with one hand, he molested me, and he used his other hand to tightly clasp my mouth shut. As tears streamed down my toddler cheeks, he ordered me to stop crying, for fear that my tears and sobbing would cause my mom to wake up. During this time, I thought that I would suffocate and/or die. Nights were filled with fear of the unknown. "Would it happen again? Would he hurt me again? Would my mom find out? Would I get into trouble? Would she be able to help me stop him from hurting me? When would I ever be able to sleep again?" I asked myself these questions over and over each night as I wrapped my blankets tightly around me at bedtime. Bob did this over and over again. He told me that if I told my mom what was going on, he would hurt her. It was here that I learned to *keep secrets.* There were a couple of times when Bob woke me up in the middle of the night, if I fought him, he would roll my body up and place me in the clothes dryer. I was a dainty little thing, so for him, this was no trouble at all. The dryer was my dungeon. He once turned the dryer on, but for only a second, just to scare me. I remember pounding my little fists against the walls of the inside of the dryer. That literally took my breath away. He opened the dryer door to ask me if I had had enough. I had no words to answer him back, so with sobs, I would shake my head yes. He would then take me to my room, put me in bed and leave me there, for *that* night. I could never seem to sleep. At night, I was always paralyzed with fear and terror! Claustrophobia entered my life here.

My baby brother, Donny was born when I was three years old. I felt like with him, I had a real-life baby doll. I would cradle him in my arms. I was a big sister! I didn't feel alone anymore. Donny held me captive with his utter cuteness. His hearty giggles, chubby little cheeks and his soft blue eyes all made me feel like the world around me could be perfect, but I also felt a strange sense of needing to be his protector. I never wanted him to be far from me.

My mom, Bob, Donny and I often went to the frog jump water area at a lake near the Pacific Ocean. Bob had a thrill for the water and he liked frogs. He would find frogs and have them race on a track that he would make in the sand. I enjoyed going there, because it was so open and when he would be busy with the frogs, my mom, Donny and I would play in the sand and wet our feet in the waves. It was so much fun! It was never really crowded where we would be.

One particular time, when I was four and a half years old, we were in a secluded area near the ocean. It was just us four with the ocean to ourselves. While my mom, Bob & Donny were on a picnic blanket enjoying a late lunch, I decided to trail off on my own and make my way to the edge of the water. As I was playing in the waves, a wave overtook me and threw me out into the ocean. I screamed my heart out for help and became disoriented. During this time, my big toe on my right foot became stuck in a hole in the bottom of the ocean. I was only about three feet out, but in my little mind I was forever away from my mom. The hole that I was caught in felt like it was a circle of glass. I was stuck! My arms were waving in violent jerks as I vigorously bobbed in and out of the water, screaming with all of my might for my mom to come and rescue me. Through the crashing waves, I could see my mom being held down by Bob and my baby brother was screaming. I felt completely helpless. Suddenly, Bob screamed at me, "Call me Daddy and I will come and get you out of the water!"

Blood curdling screams came out of my mouth. "Call *him* daddy??? No!!" I told myself. My mom was trying to pull herself from him but she couldn't free herself from his grip. All at once, I felt these huge arms pull me up out of the water and set me on the sandy beach. I was safe. My foot was covered in blood as I ran with all of my might, tripping every few steps while I favored my right foot and finally made it into the arms of my mom. Once I reached her, I collapsed in her arms. My cries were uncontrollable. My mom pulled herself free from Bob's hands, grabbed me in her arms and rocked me. As she did this, she yelled at Bob for not getting me out of the water and for not allowing her to get me out of the water.

He screamed out, "All she had to do was call me Daddy!" It was then that I looked for the person who had brought me out of the water. There was no one around. Absolutely no one! All I knew was that the person who pulled me out of the water was someone big and someone who had a lot of strength. I wondered to myself if it could have been an angel who pulled me out.

My mom and Bob spent a lot of time drinking with friends and smoking marijuana. My brother and I spent those times playing in our bedroom together, so we weren't in the way. The house was always loud with music and people. We lived in a duplex in San Jose, California. The neighbors, who were an older couple would often come over and ask for my mom and Bob to keep the noise down. They always said that they would, but would often just keep the parties going. After the company would leave, my brother and I would come out of the bedroom and find our mom and Bob asleep either on the floor or on the couch. The house smelled awful and it was a disaster. They would sleep for what seemed like forever.

One night, in the middle of the night, I heard whimpering. At first, I thought that I was dreaming about it. After rubbing my eyes to wake myself up though, I realized that it was the whimper of my little brother. I got up quickly and went down the hall and opened the *closet room* door. When I did this, I saw my brother with his clothes off and Bob with his pants off holding my brother close to him. My brother was crying and trying to pull himself away from Bob. I ran in and yanked at my brother trying to free him from Bob's grip. Bob glared at me and without saying a word, got up and got dressed. My brother slept with me that night. I don't know where my mom was during those terrorizing nights. If she was home, I wondered if she could hear us crying. I also wondered if she had any idea what Bob was doing.

Somehow, I learned how to change my brother's diapers, so I did that often. I looked through cupboards for something for us to eat. It was usually bread, crackers, candy, or dry dog food that I would find. We were thrilled with whatever it was that we were able to find and we devoured it.

Sometimes the four of us would sit on our couch and watch tv together or maybe walk to the park. Donny and I loved to be twirled around the merry-go-round. We also loved to hear the ice cream truck turn the corner. We would all run to it and we were thrilled to get orange push up ice creams. Bob always had a pocketful of change for us to use at the ice cream truck. Actually, I don't know who was more excited for the ice cream truck to come, my brother and I, or my mom and Bob? These moments didn't come very often, so when they did, I soaked in all of the fun that I could.

My mom and Bob never married. They argued a lot, though I never saw it. Sometimes I heard him yelling at her and hitting her and her trying to keep her cries from us. One morning when I got up, Bob was just gone. I never asked where he was. I have often wondered what my mom ever saw in him.

My mom, Donny and I lived in Oakland, California for a short time. It was not a safe neighborhood. I was now in kindergarten and was teased a lot, because I was the only *white* girl in the school. We had to go up stairs to get to the front door of our house. The large horizontal living room window faced the front yard and street. There were often times that my mom would ask me to go down to the corner store and get some things for her. Things like milk, bread, beef jerky. I didn't want to go, but she begged me and she promised that she would watch me from the window while I walked there and back. I didn't like going, because every time I went outside horrible things would be screamed at me by our neighbors. Racial comments were shouted out at me and glass bottles were thrown at me. When I made it back to our house, my mom would be crying. She felt bad about what had gone on. She told us that one day we would not have to live there anymore.

We spent a lot of time visiting my grandparents, Grandma and Grandpa Tomasetti in Dublin, California. It was here that I felt safe. Grandma always colored with me. We would sit on her living room floor and color for hours. She taught me how to outline the pictures with a dark color and use a lighter color to color in the picture. It was always important for us to date the pictures after they were finished. There were countless coloring books and crayons stored in her coffee table. Grandma also loved painting her nails. They were always painted white. Her hair was long and auburn in color. She loved country music, especially Patsy Cline. Her afternoon shows were *The Match Game, The Phil*

Donahue tv talk show and at night time she would watch *The Tonight Show with Johnny Carson.* At night, no matter how asleep she would appear to be, if the tv was turned off, she would wake straight up and declare that she was still awake and watching *The Tonight Show.* Fireworks and loud music could be going on all around us and she would sleep soundly through it all, but wake up the instant the tv was turned off.

My Aunt Tina, Uncle Rick and Uncle Bill still lived at Grandma and Grandpa's house. Aunt Tina and Uncle Rick were fraternal twins and they were about 16 years old, Uncle Bill was about 12 years old. They made everything fun. The neighborhood was filled with teenagers. In the evenings there were many hide and go seek games and water balloon fights. They didn't mind if Donny and I would tag along with them.

My Mom, Uncle Mike and Aunt Linda were all older. Grandma had been married two different times before marrying Grandpa Tomasetti, so her kids had big age gaps. I remember Uncle Mike often coming over to visit and when he and Uncle Rick would be sent to the store to get some groceries, they would walk to the Alpha Beta grocery store that was located across a big street that was behind the cement wall of Grandma's backyard. I would tag along with them. Uncle Mike would walk around the corner and down the street to the other side of the cement wall behind Grandma's back-yard. Uncle Rick would lift me up to the top of the cement wall. There, I would sit and muster up the courage to jump into Uncle Mike's arms. He would pretend that he wasn't going to catch me, but he always did. Uncle Rick would stand on a chair, then prop himself over the cement wall and we would then make our way to the store. We enjoyed a delicious ice cream cone on the way back to Grandma's house and we always came back the same way that we left. I enjoyed spending time with them so much.

I loved having dinner at Grandma's house. In her kitchen, the walls were adorned with wood pan-eling and there was a long wooden kitchen table, perfect for our big family gatherings. She had 6 kids and two of those 6 kids had 2 kids each, so the table would always be full. So much laughter was shared at that table. The grandkids always thought that the best part of going to Grandma and Grandpa's was the cookie jar on the far right of the kitchen counter. She would allow us to lift our-selves onto the counter and with great anticipation, very carefully lift the lid of that big brown cookie jar and take out a delicious Hydrox Oreo cookie. We savored every bit, gently turning the two sides of the cookie, carefully trying not to separate the sweet cream filling. As I ate it, it felt as though my insides were dancing.

Something that I didn't enjoy at Grandma and Grandpa's house was their front yard. It looked like a desert because of the cactus plants that had been planted throughout. There was a time that one of my uncles was spinning me around and accidentally let go of my arms a bit too early, causing me to land in the cactus. That was painful! It took a couple of days to remove all of the *invisible* cactus spines from my legs and torso. After that, I steered clear of those cactus plants!

Chapter 2

THE SHATTERED YEARS

I was 5 years old when my mom met Ken. Ken was a husky 6-foot-tall man with brownish/reddish/gray, short curly hair and a mustache. He looked even larger next to my mom, who was a dainty 5'2". After they married, we lived in Castro Valley, California. Ken was much older than my mom. My mom was 24 years old and Ken was 45. He seemed to have it all together. He was well known, as far as my mom knew. Everywhere they went together, people either knew Ken or knew of him. He had 2 grown daughters, Tina and Tammy. We didn't see them very often. Ken told me once that Tammy was in a home for girls because she was bad. I don't know how true that was. I only remember seeing her and Tina a few times. Tammy was 16 years old and Tina was 19 years old.

It appeared to many that Ken could do just about anything–cook, fix cars, play guitar. He had a drafting table and he appeared to draw on it often. He loved to enter contests, especially eating contests. He won many ice cream eating contests. He was proud when the ice cream parlor put his picture up as the All Time Winner of eating the most ice cream in the shortest amount of time. At Christmas time, he played the role of a jolly Santa Claus to many underprivileged kids. He was really good at it. I wondered why he couldn't be that jolly at home.

Ken had a much different side of him. He was very controlling. He would tell my mom what to cook and how to cook it. If what she cooked didn't taste good to him, he would throw it out and make her start over, no matter what time the clock said it was. We never knew what time Ken would be home from work. When he did get home, he insisted that we would be cleaned up and waiting for him at the door when he came in, and the dinner needed to be ready and warm and on the kitchen table waiting for us. If he arrived home late or if we ate before he came home and we were in bed, he would wake us up and make us watch him eat dinner, ever so slowly. We would need to clean up after him. If he arrived home 'on time' we were expected to greet him with a hug and the dinner needed to be ready and warm on the kitchen table, the four of us would eat together. We had to be careful not to pick up our food with our hands, no matter what it was that we were eating, even if it was bread or corn on the cob. If we picked up our food with our hands, or wiped our lips with our hand and not the napkin that was on our laps, he would throw our plates on the floor and make us eat *like dogs*. He made us lick up every morsel of food from our plates.

My mom was made to clean the floors on her hands and knees and at times with a toothbrush. If Ken thought they weren't clean enough, he would pour mustard and catsup on the floors and make her start over. I recall how tired she always was. Because she didn't drive, she was dependent on others to take her where she needed to go. Sometimes she would walk Donny and I to the park that was close by. We had a next-door neighbor named Ruth. She and her husband were older and didn't have any family around. My mom enjoyed visiting with them. We would often be invited over for homemade chocolate chip cookies and orange juice. At the front of Ruth's house, they had a playhouse made from wood. It looked old and had drawings on the walls of the inside, making me think that kids had played there once upon a time ago. She let Donny and I play there often. Sometimes my mom would let us stay there for a few hours. Ruth was a light-hearted jolly woman with a thunderous laugh. She also had caring eyes and arms of love. She made me feel safe.

Sometimes I thought Ruth was a disguised angel because when nights were loud, the door-bell would often ring, and it would be Ruth, with a worried look. She would walk in, pass a glare at Ken and without asking, she would cradle my brother and I in her arms and say, "I need some company, and this is just the company I need." She then scooped up Donny and I and took us to her house for the night. She would make us hot chocolate and she set the volume on the t.v. loud. I know now that it was to drown out the yelling and the fighting that was going on next door, at my house. On those nights that we stayed over-night at Ruth's house, we would wake up with our mouths watering. The delicious aroma of sizzling bacon filled the hallway to the bedroom we were in. We would get up and find Ruth in her pink robe and slippers at the stove. She had her coffee cup near her as she listened to gospel music as she flipped perfectly rounded pancakes. It was such a warm and cozy feeling. Ruth would turn around and see us looking at her with our drooling faces. She would come at us with her thunderous laugh and greet us with a devouring hug and invite us to the table. There, she and her husband and Donny and I would enjoy a scrumptious breakfast. After breakfast we would all watch cartoons together.

Our favorite cartoons to watch were Looney Tunes. Donny enjoyed the Road Runner and Bugs Bunny and I enjoyed Tweety Bird. It was so hard when we went back home. Ken pretended everything was normal, well his normal but we were always on pins and needles.

It was Ken who taught me how to ride a two-wheel bicycle. He would hold my red bike with a white banana seat in the street next to the curb as I would prop myself on it, one foot on the pedal and the other foot on the curb. He would run down the sidewalk while hanging onto the back of the seat and then he let go. It took more tries than I care to say, but after a lot of falling down, I was able to accomplish the task. Ken cheered me on and I felt so proud.

Ken liked the house dark and he would often light incense and sit on the floor in the middle of the living room, dressed in a white robe and chanting something quietly. It gave me an eerie feeling. I'm not sure where my mom was during these times. My brother and I stayed in my room.

Donny and I often played house. I would be the mom and he would be my baby. One day, we saw Ken watching us at the doorway. He looked at me and said, "You do know that you will never be anything and you will never do anything. No one will ever love you. You will probably be a drug addict and a prostitute." Then with an eerie smile he walked out of the room. I didn't feel like playing anymore, Donny and I just looked at books in my room.

There were few occasions that I recall being at a house that resembled the house of the *Full House* TV show. When that show first came out on tv, the opening of the show startled me because it looked a lot like the dreadful house Ken took us to. It was a large, two story, white house with long vertical windows on the front and a long downhill driveway. I don't recall whose house it was but there were always a lot of people there. I don't remember my mom being there.

One night while my brother and I and the other kids were there playing in an upstairs playroom, I heard chanting coming from downstairs. After a few minutes, the chanting became louder and louder and sounded rough. Curiously, I tiptoed down the stairs and peeked around the corner of the hallway, I froze at what I saw. There were about 10 people dressed in white robes. They looked like they were in a daze. A strong scent of incense filled the room. I felt fearful. There was a knock at the door. When one of the people called out for the person to come in, the person didn't come in by opening the door, but by coming through the door. My mouth dropped open as I gasped and I hid myself around the hallway corner. A few minutes later, I couldn't help myself, so I reluctantly looked again. At this time, I was shocked with disbelief when I saw a dog levitating around the living room. All the while, Ken led the group around the living room and they continued to chant deeply and loudly. They walked to the corner of the living room to the fireplace and threw something powder-like into the fire, causing the fire to expand and make a loud crackling sound. It was at this time that I ran with all of my might back to the playroom and stayed put for the rest of the night, the whole time wondering what it was that I had just seen.

Another time while we were at his house, again my brother and I, along with other kids were in the upstairs playroom. There was some remodeling being done to one of the rooms in the house, or so I thought. When I went to use the bathroom, I noticed on the way that there was a large room off to the side that had yellow caution tape on the door frame and on the closet doors. There was also a sign that boldly read, **"Keep Out!"** I wondered why the room was like that, but hurried off to get to the bathroom. On my way back however, curiosity got the best of me and my 7-year-old self decided to investigate. First though, I had to make sure no one was around. I looked around and then I went to the stairway. I could hear all of the grownups downstairs busily talking. My heart was beating out of my chest as I made my way back to the *'keep out' room, because* I was scared of getting into trouble by not following the *'keep out' rule.* I wondered to myself why I couldn't go in there. After all, the note didn't say that it was dangerous in the room. Hmmm. Well, I knew that if I was going to see what was going on in that room, I'd better do it now, before someone came upstairs and saw where I was and what I was doing. I squeezed myself between two of the middle horizontal caution taped areas. I was ever so careful not to trip. When I made it, I cautiously tiptoed in. The long closet was to the right of where I was walking. The sliding closet doors were off of the door frame and they were tilted inside the closet. I decided to peek into the closet and when I did, I gasped at what I saw. "What was it that I was seeing?", I thought to myself. I couldn't believe it. I rubbed my eyes vigorously with my shaking hands and looked again. There they were again. What was it? Three older bodies right side up. They were clothed and they were wrapped in plastic. One man and two women. I let out a scream, then I quickly covered my mouth to cover up the scream and hurried out of that 'keep out' room. I was shaking uncontrollably when I made it back to the playroom. Fear gripped me. My brother and the other kids that were in the room had no idea what I had seen. I never told anyone about this. Not until years later. In my young adulthood another TV show called *Unsolved Mysteries* was popular. I wondered if one of those *Unsolved*

Mysteries had anything to do with the bodies that were wrapped in plastic and hidden in the wall. I wish that I could recall more just to put those poor souls to rest.

One Saturday morning, thinking that my mom was in her bedroom, I knocked on her bedroom door and just as I started to enter, like I was able to do all of the other Saturday mornings, I noticed that it wasn't my mom who was lying in bed with Ken, it was his older daughter, Tina. Ken didn't see me, but Tina did. She looked at me and then she turned away. I excused myself at once and ran away to my room, shocked at what I had just seen. I thought to myself, "If he was in bed with his daughter, what was going to stop him from doing to me what Bob did to me?" Tina and I never talked about this. I don't know where my mom was during this time.

One afternoon, I heard Tina screaming at her dad in the living room. She screamed that she was pregnant with *his* child as she pounded his chest with her fists. After this, I never saw her again. There are a few nights that I remember it being late at night and very loud rock and roll music was playing in our front yard. There were several men drinking and they were sitting on their motorcycles.

Ken was in the middle of it all. When my mom went to the door to ask them to quiet down, before she could get the words out Ken told her to get herself back in the house. Those nights, my mom and my brother and I slept together in my brother's room. It was the room that was furthest away from my mom and Ken's room.

One day while my mom was cleaning the back door glass window. While she was doing this, I heard a loud crash. My mom's hand crashed through the glass window and her forearm was bleeding pretty badly. I grabbed a dishrag and she wrapped her arm in it. She had me try to call Ruth from next door to see if she could drive my mom to the hospital, but she wasn't home therefore we ran to the corner and waited for the next city bus. After my mom had stitches put in, we made our way back home, again by city bus. From here on out, it seemed like my mom was going to doctor appointments quite often.

It was just after summertime in 1975, I was starting the 3rd grade. Almost every day, Ruth would pick me up from school and take me over to her house where she was watching Donny. My mom seemed to never be around. When I would ask where my mom was, Ruth casually said that she was either busy or had a doctor appointment. When she was at home, my mom looked weak and tired, and ever so thin. She had always been thin, but now, she was skeleton thin. She didn't look well. One day I was told that she was living in the hospital. I don't recall going to see her very often.

There was something that Ken made Donny and I do just about every night before we went to bed. He had a huge velvet glow in the dark photo of the devil hanging in the hallway, right next to my bedroom door. The picture hung long ways. In this picture, the devil was sitting in a large green armchair with a cigar hanging out of his tightly closed mouth. His arms were on the arms of the chair he was in. In one hand he held a glass with what I assumed was alcohol. His other hand held a large pitchfork. His eyes were pure evil as they stared at us. All around the figure in the picture was white, gray and black smoke. It appeared to be ablaze. Ken had us stand in front of this evil picture and stare at it with our hands at our sides. We had to stare at it for about 15 minutes. If we talked or moved, Ken would have us start over again. One night, I screamed when he put me in front of that picture. I told him that it scared me and that I didn't want to look at it anymore. After snickering at me, he left for the garage and came back with some tools. He took the bolts off of my bedroom door, moved my bed near the doorway and placed a large mirror on the opposite wall that the devil picture was on. Now when I went to bed, if I looked out my bedroom door, it was that scary devil picture that I saw.

While my mom was in the hospital, Ken brought a woman and her two kids to live with us. One morning when I walked by my mom's room, I was shocked to see that the woman was dressed in my mom's clothes, wearing her jewelry and I could smell the scent of my mom's perfume—Ciara on her. I wondered who she thought she was and wondered why she was taking over all of my mom's belongings. Didn't she have her own clothes, jewelry and perfume? Her son and daughter took over all of mine and Donny's things. They slept in our rooms, wore our clothes, played with our toys and even ate at our places at the table. Donny and I wore the same clothes it seemed like every day. We slept close together on the couch every night.

When I visited my mom in the hospital, I colored while sitting close to her on her hospital bed. She mostly slept. During one of these visiting times, as I looked at her, I wondered what happened to her beautiful auburn red hair. It was gone.

My 8th birthday was celebrated with my mom at the hospital. A large room was set up with balloons, streamers, presents and a huge white cake with a ballerina on it. The room was filled with aunts, uncles, cousins, Ruth and my grandma and grandpa. It was such a fun night. My mom was happy. I was happy. My brother was happy. My most treasured birthday gift that I received that night was a small white jewelry box. When it was wound up, the ballerina spun around and around to beautiful music. I loved it.

This perfect night soon came to a screeching end. On the way home from the hospital party, as Donny and I giggled with excitement, talking about all of the fun that we had at the party, the car suddenly came to a jerking stop. We gasped and looked up at Ken wondering what had just happened. It was at this time that he glared into my eyes and snarled, "You think you are special, do you? Well, when we get home, I will show you just how special I think you are!!" Fear gripped me. I wondered what was going to happen? Donny and I held hands and we didn't say another word the rest of the ride home. When we arrived home, Ken took Donny next door, then he and I walked slowly up the walkway to our front door. I was shaking, not so much from the coldness of the air, but because of the fear that embodied me. That is when torture came. After Ken opened the front door, he threw me onto the floor, locked the door, gripped me by the hair and drug me into the bathroom. He tore off of my clothes and threw me into the bathtub. Hot water poured onto me from the shower spout as he vigorously shook my head with my hair clasped in his hands.

I screamed, "Stop, Stop, you are hurting me!" This made him do it even harder. At one point he told me not to move. I sat in the bathtub shaking, with my knees bent into my chest, my arms hugging my legs and with my face looking down into my knees, I sobbed uncontrollably. Ken went out the back door and quickly came back in. He came into the bathroom with two long thin branches from our tree and hit them against my body. Each swipe against my wet body burned. When he yanked me out of the bathtub, I had red welts on my frail fair skinned body. He then rubbed my body down with a large green towel and threw me onto my bed. When he tossed me on the bed, I bounced and hit my head on the wall that the head of my bed was up against. I let out blood curdling screams.

He yelled, "Well, if you are going to scream, then I am going to give you something to scream about." I was so scared, I didn't know what to do. My body ached. Did I dare move? I was so cold. I wanted my pajamas on.

When Ken left the room, I attempted to get up quickly to find something to put on. But just as I sat up, he walked back and yelled, "What do you think you are doing?" In a quivering voice, I said that I was cold and wanted my pajamas on.

He abruptly yanked me away from the bed and onto the floor, threw back my blankets and threw me back onto my bed and told me to "Freeze." I held my breath in fear that the motion of my chest moving on my unclothed body would cause him to hurt me again. He left the room. I heard the garage door open and then close. I wondered what he was doing. About a minute later, he was back with something in his hands. It was a circular plastic container with a lid on top of it. It was about the size of a 15-ounce butter tub. He lifted the circular tub about two inches above my bare body and snapped the lid off. That is when small spiders were poured all over me. I was too scared to scream, but my body shook uncontrollably. Ken then laid the blankets that he had earlier thrown to the side on top of me, covering even my head and tightly tucked the edges of the blankets under the bed mattress. The spiders eerily crawled over my body, between my toes, on my stomach, my inner thighs, my head, my face, everywhere. I don't recall how that night ended, but a new-found fear was born—the extreme fear of spiders, arachnophobia.

One day, as I was at the hospital getting ready to see my mom, I carried coloring books and crayons with me down the hospital hallway. When I reached her hospital door, I saw something that I had never witnessed before. There was a man at my mom's bedside sitting near her with his hands in hers. His voice was calm and reassuring. He was reading the Bible to her and she was smiling as she was listening to him. I also heard him pray with her. At the end of his prayer, I heard him pray "...and Lord, please be with Judy and keep her two precious kids safe, in Jesus Name I pray, Amen." When he left the room, he smiled a warm smile, winked at me and patted my head. I hoped that I would see this kind man again.

I soon learned that this kind man was a Preacher. I saw him a few other times and each time, he always wore a kind smile and he was always gentle, and he always prayed with my mom.

A short time later, Grandma and Grandpa's house was different as my mom was now living in one of the bedrooms at their house. Grandma later told me that she didn't want my mom to spend her last days in the hospital, but at home with her, so she could take care of her.

Chapter 3

SECURITY LOST

On December 21, 1975, after Ken had finished playing the jolly role of Santa Claus at a big gathering and as we started our drive home, Donny and I were sucking on our candy canes in the backseat of the car when Ken turned his face toward us and said, "By the way, your mom's dead!" That was it. That was all he said. He then turned up the radio and drove us home.

"What? My mom was gone? Forever?" I wondered what was going to happen to us. I wondered if we were going to be sent away to a *troubled kids* home, like Tammy was. We cried. We were scared. We held tightly onto each other. Cancer had taken my mom from me.

That night, Ken again had us stare at that devil picture in the hallway. Again, we stood as still as we could, with tears streaming down our broken faces. But, this night when we looked at the picture, it wasn't the evil that I saw. I saw a bright light and a figure of a man's face, and I heard the words, "Not much longer, you will be safe." The voice didn't startle me at all, I felt calm. I didn't know who or what it was that I saw and heard in the picture, but I did know that it was the opposite of the evil and darkness that I had come to know.

My mom was buried on Christmas Eve 1975. It was an open casket. When we were taken to view her, I didn't recognize her at all. I wondered if a trick was being played on me. I wondered if Ken had taken my mom away and hid her from me, because he had threatened to do that before. As I looked at everyone around me, I knew that my aunts, uncles and my grandma and grandpa wouldn't be there if it wasn't true. Grandma was devastated. Her cries were at times uncontrollable.

Ken still had the woman and her kids living in our house and taking over all of our things. I am thankful that he did take us to see Grandma often. I enjoyed being with her so much. But now, things were different. She was always sad. There were many times that she would take me into her room and we would sit on her bed and look through a small box together. The box held memories of my mom. There were some photos, a couple of report cards, a turquoise silver ring and her dainty soft pink slippers with a flower cluster by the toes. Each item held the scent of my mom. As Grandma carefully reached for them, she would caress them, raise them to her cheek one at a time and as a tear ran down her cheek, she kissed each item as she placed them carefully back into the box and put the lid back on. We would talk about my mom and just lay together. After a while, we got up and placed the box in the back left of the top shelf in the closet of the room that my mom had once been in.

In January of 1976, Ken received a call from my Aunt Linda. She asked if she could have Donny and I over for a weekend. Ken didn't mind at all. In fact, he told her that she could have us that upcoming weekend. Donny and I were so excited. We loved Aunt Linda. She had a man in her life that she lived with, his name was Joe. They lived together with her two kids, Lisa and Tony and his two kids, Ginger and Joey. Lisa was 13 years old, Tony was 12, Ginger was 7 and Joey was 5. Donny and I fit right in, he was 5 and I was 8. We had fun being with them. They lived in Hayward, California right next door to the Rotten Robbie gas station, across the street from a Fire Station and caddy corner to Mt. Eden High School. There was also a bus stop in front of the house. The house had two front yards with a short cement wall that sep-arated the two yards, and there was a gate that had a latch in the middle of the long cement wall. I learned that there were two front yards, because it was a high traffic area. Aunt Linda and Uncle

Joe said they wanted the kids to have a safe area to play out front. When you walked into the house, there was a front-front room, which was filled with bikes, outdoor equipment and boxes. This room led to the living room. It was a long living room. It was set up with a long couch, loveseat and recliner chair, a long coffee table and two big bean bags, one for each of the dogs. Misty was a blind German shepherd and not afraid of anything. She could catch fish in the water, birds in the air and even jump over the fence without any problems. Brandy, who was a Labrador with adorable floppy ears, was not as brave as Misty. He was afraid of everything. They each had their own big bean bag chairs right near the living room fireplace. They also had a Siamese cat, Gibby who was rather bossy. She didn't have any problem scatting unwelcomed people or animals away from her. The living room had an opening in the back that led to the kitchen area. There were four stools set in front of the counter facing the kitchen. The kitchen was to the right of the living room. There was a table area and a counter space that separated the cooking area and the dining area. By the kitchen entryway was a small coat closet and a wall heater. Tony and Joey shared a bedroom across from the kitchen and a few steps down the hall, Lisa and Ginger shared a bedroom. Both rooms had bunk beds and two dressers. One dresser was placed in the closets and one would be near the bed in each of the rooms. Aunt Linda and Joe's master bedroom and bathroom was across from the girls' bedroom and the main bathroom was at the end of the hall. The house was small for six people, but they made it work.

On Sunday, mid-morning of that weekend, after Donny and I had spent the day with Aunt Linda and Uncle Joe and all of the kids shopping at a flea market, we drove up to the house and the front yard was covered with boxes and...my bike. I wondered what was going on. All 6 of us kids were told to go into the house. I was told later that Ken was parked at the next-door gas station and when he saw the kids go into the house, he went up to Aunt Linda and told her that he didn't want us anymore and then he left. I am sure she felt help- less. What was she going to do now? They already had 4 kids, how were they going to provide for 6 kids? Then the thought left her. She knew what she had to do. She and Uncle Joe gathered all of our things and brought them into the house. Aunt Linda and Uncle Joe called us to their room and told us that Ken wasn't coming back for us and that we would be staying with them. We all hugged each other. I thought back to the kind man that I saw in the evil devil picture and that ever so calm voice that told me that not much longer, Donny and I would be safe.

Chapter 4

A New and Different Kind of Normal

Although it was crowded at Aunt Linda and Uncle Joe's house, Donny and I were able to fit into the bedrooms and more chairs were added to the round kitchen table. I was enrolled in Eureka Elementary School as a 3rd grader. I was the poster child of who to tease. I was a shy and awkward 3rd grader. I was extremely skinny, had freckles and bad buck teeth. I was a mess. And now, I needed to start a new school? Aunt Linda walked me up to my classroom that first day. I was so embarrassed. Everyone's eyes seemed to be on me. It didn't help me at all when Aunt Linda decided to introduce me as her niece and told everyone that my mom had recently died and that I needed some friends. I wanted to hide under a rock. I know that she meant well. I even knew it then, but I sure was embarrassed.

I always kept to myself, especially during my elementary school years. In 5th grade, I had a teacher named Ms. Peggy Robinson. She was not only pretty, she was kind and she noticed me. Her hair was dark brown and she mostly wore it up, her skin was soft beige. The first week of my 5th grade year, she asked me to stay after school. I wondered if I was in trouble. It turned out that she just wanted to talk. She asked me about myself. After about a month of school, she talked to Aunt Linda and asked her if she could have me over for brunch on Saturday. Of course, Aunt Linda agreed to it. Ms. Robinson lived about 5 minutes from our house. She was not married, nor did she have any kids. She taught me how to sew, she helped me with my homework, she invested in me. I was so excited when I found out that she was also going to be my 6th grade teacher. Our Saturday brunches were about six times for two years. By the time my 6th grade year was over, I knew that I wanted to one day become a teacher.

Aunt Linda took us to Grandma and Grandpa's often. Grandma would still color with me and I would still climb the counter with great anticipation in hopes of finding a cookie inside the cookie jar. Grandma still missed my mom a lot. She would often invite me to her bedroom and we would sit on her bed and look through the little box that held some of my mom's things. Grandma added items to the memory box. It now not only held the dainty light pink satin slippers and silver band turquoise ring, it also held letters that my mom wrote to her, a hanky, a Bible and a few pictures. Grandma cried when she took out each item. We quietly looked through it for maybe ten minutes, put it away and then went about doing other things. I loved doing this with her.

At the time, I wasn't sure of the reason behind it, but one late summer, Lisa talked all of us kids into running away. Lisa was 13 years old, Tony was 12, I was 9, Ginger was 8 and Joey and Donny were 6. She called a meeting and declared that we were all going to go on an adventure. She said that it would be fun, because we were all going to do it together. She said that we all needed to pack pillowcases up with food and clothes. We all slept in our clothes and early the next morning, it was a Saturday, we woke up at 5 am and were ready to go. Suddenly though, on the way out of the house, I decided that it wasn't such a good idea. Lisa told me that I didn't have any choice and she reminded me that we had already agreed to do this together.

All night I had thought about *the plan*. I thought that it would be scary. I thought that it would be cold, especially at night. I knew this because it was decided that we would be following a path to the Salt Flats near Hayward. I wondered what we were going to do after we got there? I knew that Aunt Linda would be scared and worried. I didn't want to go. I begged Lisa to let me stay home. She again said that I had to, because we were all doing this together. After more begging, she demanded that I not tell Aunt Linda and Uncle Joe about *the plan*. I told her I wouldn't, while I crossed my fingers behind my back. I begged Donny not to go, but he was an adventurous 6-year-old and he wanted to go. They all made their move and left. Now what was I going to do? I was beginning to second guess my decision. All I could do now was think about what I was going to tell Aunt Linda and Uncle Joe when they discovered that 5 of their 6 kids were gone.

I heard Aunt Linda get up for a cup of coffee at about 10 am She wondered out loud why it was so quiet. She knocked on the boys bedroom door, calling, "Wake up sleepy heads." She didn't get an answer. She knocked on the girls' bedroom door. Again, no answer. She quietly opened the door and saw just me. I was lying on the bottom bunk bed. She asked me where all of the other kids were. I told her that I didn't know. (Well, really,

I didn't know what they were doing at that specific time, I told myself, condoning the lie that I had just told). I heard her walk through the house and call out for them. She looked in the backyard and then the front yard. No sign of them. My heart was beating so fast. Aunt Linda finally decided that maybe the kids went across the street to the high school to play some ball.

After 2 hours, because Aunt Linda thought that they would be home for sure by now, because they were always hungry, she decided to go to the high school to look for them. Uncle Joe was now very worried. I was pacing and pacing. When Aunt Linda came back saying that she didn't see them, I couldn't take it any longer. After taking a deep breath, I blurted out, "They ran away!" They both looked at me in shock asking if I was serious and why I didn't say anything earlier about it. I told them that I was sworn to secrecy. Apparently, Lisa had gotten herself into some kind of trouble and instead of facing her punishment on Saturday, she thought of another plan that involved all of us. By late afternoon, there was still no sign of them. I felt horrible. What if something happened to them? Then it would be all my fault. I then asked myself why I didn't just tell Aunt Linda and Uncle Joe sooner? Like soon after they had left, after all Lisa couldn't get mad at me if she didn't make it back safely.

The police were called and were on the lookout for 5 runways, ages 6 through 13. Thankfully, they were found Sunday afternoon by the police. They were dirty, hungry and had head lice. But, they were safe!

Donny and I sometimes spent weekends with our Uncle Mike and Aunt Claudia. They lived in a duplex in Oakland. They didn't have any kids, but they did have a dog that they treated like a child. His name was Midnight. Uncle Mike and Aunt Claudia were simple people. I loved spending time with them. They made me feel extremely loved and really safe. Aunt Claudia would often braid Uncle Mike's long hair and I loved it when she taught me how to braid my hair. They didn't drive and they loved their 70's music. We would go on walks together to the nearby market. On the way, there was a 3-foot cement wall and every time we passed that wall Uncle Mike would tell Donny and I to get ready to watch him scale over the cement wall without even touching it. We eagerly watched and each time, Uncle Mike either tripped on the way over the wall or toppled over after his stomach hit the top of the wall. It would cause him to laugh and in turn get us giggling. I am sure that he must have hurt himself more than a few times after doing it. But each time we visited, he always did it again. We also watched movies, ate junk food and we spent a lot of time at the park. They had a friend named Rocky who would usually go with us. Rocky had a dog too. He had rescued the dog after he had seen people throwing broken glass bottles at him and hitting him. One day when we were at the park, there was a dog fight going on. Rocky decided that he was going to try to stop it. As he put his hand in the middle of the fight, a dog bit off one of his fingers. It was awful to watch. He came over to our picnic area and took the ice bag out of the ice chest and covered his hand with it. Someone who had been with us took him to the hospital. Before they left, a man came up to him with a cup and told Rocky that what was in the cup was his. It was his finger. The finger could not be reattached. I never forgot that story. Since that day, I have always greeted animals with a closed fist, instead of an open hand to their nose to try to prevent myself from getting a finger bitten off.

Uncle Joe had a Great Aunt, her name was Verla, we called her Auntie Verla. She lived in Alameda, California. She was older and her husband, Cleo passed away in 1974, they didn't have any kids. Auntie Verla was a retired nurse and she had her mom, Maude living with her. Ma's health had been declining and Auntie Verla cared for her. Auntie Verla loved to sew. Every holiday she sewed our family table cloths, kitchen towels, dish rags, and table runners. She also sewed quilts for everyone in the family. I still have mine. It is a mix of pink and blue with a rickrack design and it has her name stitched in. She also enjoyed crocheting. She taught Aunt Linda how to crochet. They crocheted scarves, mittens, slippers and beanie hats. Auntie Verla also made the most absolutely delicious homemade chocolate chip cookies ever. Every time we went over there. Before we even reached her front door, we could smell them. She made dozens and dozens of them, allowing us to take some home with us.

Auntie Verla loved elephants. She had a collection of them throughout her house. Aunt Linda always made sure that each gift that we gave to Auntie Verla had an elephant to go with it. Aunt Linda had a love for ducks, so Auntie Verla would reciprocate by enclosing a duck with each gift that she gave to Aunt Linda.

All six of us kids loved playing in Auntie Verla's basement. It was like a second house. It had a kitchen and a large living room and one bedroom and one bathroom. The floors were cement and there were two windows that faced a beautifully landscaped backyard of roses that made a nice view. Auntie Verla never went into the basement. Ginger and I loved to go down there and fix it up with boxes and assorted items to make it feel like a house. We also took a radio down there and just sat and played checkers or cards.

Alameda is about a half hour from Hayward. When it looked like we were going to go see Auntie Verla, Ginger and I secretly packed a change of clothes and hid them in the station wagon. When Aunt Linda would be getting ready for us to go home, Ginger and I begged to stay overnight with Auntie Verla. At first it took a lot of talking to get Aunt Linda to agree, but after a while of doing this every time we went, she knew the asking would come, so she had already planned on us staying. She seemed to enjoy hearing us beg. Auntie Verla didn't drive, so Aunt Linda always came back to get us the next day, which she enjoyed because spending time with Auntie Verla was one of her most favorite things to do.

Auntie Verla would take Ginger and I to South Shore, which is an outdoor shopping mall, almost every time that we stayed with her. We took the city bus. We always stopped at Woolworth's, which was a department store/diner. First, we would sit on the stools that were at the counter and enjoy BLT's and milkshakes and then we would buy nail polish. Afterwards, we strolled around the outdoor shopping mall and sometimes we would cross the street and walk on the waterfront, which is a part of the San Francisco Bay. Three hours later, we caught the bus back to Auntie Verla's house.

Auntie Verla had a long stereo console in her living room, which included a record player, an 8-track tape player and a radio. We loved playing country music. We listened to Tanya Tucker, Donny and Marie Osmond and Shaun Cassidy records. We made pretend microphones out of paper rolled up long ways and sang to the music as loud as we could. Auntie Verla sang with us. We laughed and laughed. We stayed up late and woke up late. In the morning, Auntie Verla always made hash browns and scrambled eggs with toast and orange juice.

One Christmas morning, the six of us kids woke up in the wee hours of the morning with great anticipation of what we would find under the Christmas tree. Very quietly, we tiptoed into the living room and were completely dismayed to see that there was *NOTHING* under the Christmas tree. Not one gift. Our ages ranged from about 6 -14 years old. Lisa knocked on Aunt Linda's bedroom door and told her that there weren't any gifts under the tree. Aunt Linda sprung out of bed and told her to tell us to get something to eat while she went to the bathroom and she would come and see what had happened. We reluctantly ate our cereal. While we did that, Aunt Linda hurriedly called Auntie Verla and told her what had happened. She had bought all of the gifts, but they were still in the trunk of our car, *not wrapped.* She asked Auntie Verla to call back and pretend that she was Santa Claus, who was running late because of a sled mishap. When she hung the telephone up she told us that Santa called and said that he was on his way, but we needed to go to bed and pretend to be asleep so he would come. Of course, we wanted him to come, so to bed we went. Lisa and Tony played along. They were old enough to know better. Aunt Linda rushed to the car, took out all of the gifts and hurriedly wrapped them, tagged them and placed them under the tree. She did this in record time, about 45 minutes. Then, out of breath she went and *woke* us up. Aunt Linda didn't share this story with me until years later. Every Christmas when we talked about it, it always brought back good memories.

As we all got older, we still enjoyed spending time with Auntie Verla. She was a big part of our lives. Aunt Linda and Auntie Verla talked often on the telephone. Because the calls were long distance, Aunt Linda would have Auntie Verla call our home and let it ring one time and then hang up. She would then call Auntie Verla back and they would talk for hours. Uncle Joe didn't like long distance calls to be made, but when it came to calls to Auntie Verla, he never complained. They would usually talk on Sundays when the rates were less expensive.

In 1980, I was 12 years old and I was finally able to get braces. I had to have nine teeth pulled all on the same day. Knowing that, you could probably imagine how bad my teeth were. I had too many teeth for my little mouth. Now, I was shy, skinny, freckled and had a brace face, with a neck gear. I became the brunt of many jokes. Grandma was so excited after I got my braces. She said that she could only imagine how good my teeth were going to look and that she looked forward to me not hiding my smiles anymore. She said that she was going to take me to a nice dinner the day my braces came off. However, she would never be able to see that happen, because she made her way to heaven that September. Emphysema cut her life short, she was 49 years old. I was 12 years old and I was devastated. She was the closest person to me that reminded me of my mom. She had suffered a lot with her illness. Uncle Bill, who at the time was 16 years old and the last of Grandma's 6 kids to still be at home spent much of his time taking care of Grandma and making sure she had her oxygen and that she was comfortable. That was a lot for him to take on. He should have been having the time of his life, enjoying his high school years, and his girlfriend, Sherri, whom he later married.

About a year after Grandma passed away, our family was at my grandma and grandpa's house sitting around the table. All of the kids were either watching tv or playing outside. When I walked into the kitchen, I heard them talking about how Grandma at times would talk vaguely about some things that had belonged to my mom. They were asking each other if they knew where those items were. No one did. I spoke up that I knew where my mom's things were. "You Do?" Uncle Rick asked. I answered him, "Yes." He asked me to show them where they were. I led them all into the bedroom that my mom had spent her last days and pushed a chair next to the opened closet door. As I stood on the chair, I pointed to the back-left side of the shelf. There were blankets covering the small box. Uncle Rick reached up and pulled the box down from the shelf. He took the lid off and everyone gasped and Uncle Rick said, "So, *that* is where Grandma put the box." Hearing him say that made my heart swell. I felt so very special. I was the only person that Grandma shared those memories with. They gave me the pink slippers and the turquoise silver ring from the box. They were not only memories of my mom now, but also memories of my grandma.

Our family of 8 was nothing like the family of 8 on The Brady Bunch. Yes, there were 3 girls and 3 boys and a mom and dad, but that is where the similarities ended. As we all grew up, we were all growing out of our little 1,200 square foot house, which made tensions high at times. Uncle Joe, who worked as a mechanic, building engines for race cars pulled his back out, which caused him to have herniated discs. After having surgery and after going through much rehabilitation he was able to gain back limited mobility, however he still experienced back pain and had back spasms more often than not. He was miserable. He had to stop working, but he still worked in his garage rebuilding engines for people at his own pace and they would pay him for it. In the garage, everything except the washer and dryer belonged to him. He had every tool imaginable and he had numerous fishing gear. Everything had its place. He was very meticulous about keeping his things in order. He spent a lot of time in the garage. Often, because I thought he would be lonely, I would go out in the garage with a book and sit close by him on a stool and read. Sometimes we would talk, but most times I would just be there while he worked. He always enjoyed listening to Conway Twitty on the radio.

We had more ups than downs living with Aunt Linda and Uncle Joe. All three boys played baseball each summer and that kept our family busy working at the snack bar and cheering Tony, Joey and Donny on.

Lisa had the gift of playing the guitar and she had a beautiful voice. She would often lead the family in singing songs. Her choice of songs were from the groups- Journey, Def Leppard, Styx and Led Zeppelin. At times we would all join together and do talent shows for Aunt Linda and Uncle Joe and their friends. We all worked on a tree house in the backyard for a few years. The funny thing about it though was that by the time it was finished either we lost interest in it or we grew too big to enjoy it.

Our family didn't have a lot of money however there was a lot of love. Aunt Linda and Uncle Joe made sure that we spent time together having fun as often as we could. Because they loved the outdoors so we were able to go camping at least three different times each summer. We would camp at North Shore Lake Camanche in Ione, California and Don Pedro Lake in Tuolumne County, California and a campground that was called Shads. The drive to Shads was about 2 hours from our home in Hayward. We took our green Chevy truck that had a camper shell. Seatbelts were not a law at this time, and it is a good thing, because all six of us kids were allowed to take a friend camping with us. That made 12 kids/teens in the back camper. It was set up great, we thought. A cassette radio was installed in the back and there was a large board set up sort of like a bunk bed. Some of us could relax on the top, while the others sat below. We thought it was awesome. Two or more families would follow us. When we arrived at our campground, it would be mid-morning. We all worked together to set up our tents and unpack the ice chests, food, etc. We couldn't wait to make our way to the campground store/snack bar. We were always greeted by an older woman that went by the name of Effie. The twelve of us kids enjoyed a Shirley Temple drink and chips. Uncle Joe would get his fishing tackle. Effie always gave him a good deal and then we would make our way back to the campground where Aunt Linda and all of the other women would be drinking beer, relaxing and enjoying the great outdoors.

We loved to go swimming in the pond. In the middle of the pond, there was a large wooden deck that we would all swim to and then tire ourselves out by jumping in, diving in and doing flips into the water. There was also a big tree close by the pond that had a thick rope tied to the core branch that was bolted into the tree. Everyone, except me, because I was not at all brave enough to even try, enjoyed taking turns swinging off of that rope and catapulting into the water. Tony always won at making the biggest splash.

We also enjoyed finding the blackberry patches at Shads. We would take buckets with us to gather the blackberries. Because we would snack on them, we always came back to the campground covered in the blackberry juice. They were so ripe with flavor.

During one of our camping trips at Shads, everyone in our campground decided to go for a walk. We were enjoying the sound of the river that was close by and the outdoors was so rich in color. As we were walking on the green grass, we suddenly heard a crunch. All at once, the ground was now covered in red and red specks were flying all around us–in our hair, on our faces, on our clothes. They were everywhere. We had walked into an area where ladybugs had migrated. We had to squint our eyes, cover our ears and our nostrils the best that we could with our hands and fingers and keep our mouths tightly closed. As we rushed our way back to our campground, every step we took were loud crunches. Our campground had ladybugs all around it, but nothing compared to the migrated area. Later on in my life, people questioned if this had really happened. When they heard the stories from people that had been there, they realized that it was indeed true.

Sometimes our family would go to the Hayward Regional Shoreline in Alameda County. It was so cold there. We went early in the morning at around 6 am, Uncle Joe said that time was the very best time to go fishing, because that was the time that the fish were always hungry. He caught countless bass fish. He enjoyed the quiet. One morning, as we were there fishing, I was shocked that I actually had something bite my hook. It pulled and pulled on my hook. I held on with all of my might and with excitement called out that I thought I had caught a fish. Uncle Joe hurried over the best that he could. At first, he tried to help me reel in the fish, but when the fish looked like it was going to get the best of us, he yanked the fishing pole out of my hand and after much force pulled out a 4-foot shark. "A Shark??", Uncle Joe exclaimed. "Patti, honey, Congratulations! You just caught a shark! Way to go!" I was shockingly surprised. I had never caught anything before, so why not catch a shark? That shark was just about as tall as me! I felt really proud about that!

Because I was so gullible, Uncle Joe got a big kick out of telling me stories. One specific story that he told me over and over is, "Don't ever wear red polish on your toes, because sharks are most attracted to that color. They might nibble at your toes." Whenever I am near the ocean, I still think about his fable.

Out of all six of us kids, four of us had birthdays in the month of November. Every week of the month came a birthday. Aunt Linda started a tradition. She would allow each of us to take our birthdate off from school and she would take the birthday person to breakfast or lunch and then they would get to choose whatever they wanted for the family dinner. Growing up, my favorite place to eat was McDonald's, so it was McDonald's that I chose. Little did my family know, when my birthday came, the McDonalds that was located by our house had an anniversary special during that week and hamburgers were only 10 cents each. You can only imagine the deal that was for our family of eight- and the surprise on the faces of the people when we would order 30 hamburgers and if we had friends or extended family with us we always ordered more.

Our house was always busy. Aunt Linda and Uncle Joe had big hearts. If there was any family or any friends that needed a place to stay, our door was always open. Every night, Aunt Linda always made enough food for an army, because their friends always stopped by around dinner time. And there was always *just* enough food for everyone. There were quite a few times that a family of five would stay with us until they were able to get back on their feet again.

Aunt Linda and I were very close. We enjoyed spending time together. When she would run errands, she would ask all of the kids if anyone wanted to ride along with her. When everyone would say no, I didn't want for her to be alone, so I would go. After a while, I just guessed that she would want company each time to go with her, so I was ready. However, one day she let me know that sometimes she really did want to be alone and enjoy the quietness. One of her favorite *happy places* to go to was to the nearby airport. She once told me that she enjoyed watching airplanes land and takeoff and imagine where people were going or where they had been.

There were many times that I would go into Aunt Linda's room to say goodnight and she would be in her bed watching tv. We would end up having long conversations, until we fell asleep. Uncle Joe always got a kick out of that.

When Aunt Linda and Uncle Joe brought Donny and I into their home, it was not only an act of pure unselfishness, but it also allowed us to have a sense of normalcy. Never did I wonder what might happen to me in the middle of night. We always had clothes that were our own and we never had to worry about how we ate at the dinner table, other than saying, "Please," and "Thank you."

Aunt Linda and Uncle Joe took a mini vacation to Reno, California in 1978 and were married at a wedding chapel. Aunt Linda loved Elvis Presley, so Uncle Joe made sure there was an Elvis Impersonator there. He sang for them. Aunt Linda loved Elvis so much that she had a huge velvet Elvis Presley picture hanging in our living room.

Although Aunt Linda and Uncle Joe provided a lot of love, support and security, they did have their share of marital problems. They kept a lot of things from each other. Uncle Joe had a drinking problem and Aunt Linda had a spending problem. His choice of drink was Canadian Mist with Pepsi Cola. Aunt Linda was not always honest about her shopping. Not that she was spending it on herself, she spent it on us kids. She had a habit of saving all of her receipts and balancing her checkbook at the end of each month and each month she would realize that she was missing a receipt or two and not be able to balance it correctly. Uncle Joe would be angry and she would be defensive. Other than that, I really don't know what they argued about, but when they did argue, it would become a screaming match and due to the drinking, it at times became unsafe. There were quite a few occasions that Aunt Linda packed up Lisa, Tony, Donny and I and we would either stay at an apartment with her good friend, Shelley or rent a small shack that didn't have electricity and had an outhouse for a bathroom. Sometimes when they would separate, Aunt Linda would take us to Great America in Santa Clara, California or Marine World, now known as Discovery Kingdom in Vallejo, California. Those were fun places to go, but Aunt Linda was always sad. Each time, after about two–three weeks, Aunt Linda and Joe made up and things were good, until the next time.

Chapter 5

MY INTRODUCTION TO CHRIST

One Sunday morning, while the six of us kids were in the front yard playing, Aunt Linda and Uncle Joe were replacing their king size waterbed mattress and they threw the old waterbed mattress out on the grass. We decided to patch it up, put water in it and put it in the front yard and jump on it, roll on it and jump off of it. The neighbor kids soon joined us. At one point, due to being tired out, as I was sitting on the curb, a JOY (Jesus first, Others second, Yourself last) Church bus drove by. My shy self decided to wave it down and when it stopped in front of me, I asked them if I could go with them. They said sure, but I would need to get permission from my parents. If I had their permission then they would pick me up the next week. I asked Aunt Linda and Uncle Joe about going on the JOY bus and they okayed it. The following Sunday, the JOY bus picked me up.

I was also picked up for Wednesday night church. I loved going. There were a lot of kids and the youth leaders were so much fun. My Sunday School Teacher was Betty Anglin. I called her Ms. Betty. She was older than the youth leaders. She taught me about the Bible. She brought the Bible to life by having us act out the stories. Soon after going to church and learning about Jesus and the importance of being baptized, at 11 years old I decided to get baptized. I knew now that no matter what, God was with me and that one day I would have a forever home in heaven and I would get to see my mom and my grandma again.

In the summertime, the JOY Bus took all of the kids to Great America or we would pack up and go to the park for a picnic or swimming at one of the leaders homes. Sometimes Lisa, Tony, Ginger, Joey and Donny all came along. Aunt Linda and Uncle Joe enjoyed those times, because it meant that they had a quiet house and it gave them time together. Soon after I started attending church, Aunt Linda and Uncle Joe and the rest of the kids joined me, which was wonderful, but unfortunately that only lasted for about six months or so and then for reasons unknown to me, they stopped.

After a long battle that was a bg stress on our family, Uncle Joe won a settlement over his back injury that he received while working. One of the first things that our family of eight did after the settlement was take a trip to Disneyland. Uncle Joe used a cane and moved pretty slowly throughout Disneyland. I was terrified of all of the fast rides, so I didn't mind staying close to him. I didn't want him to be lonely and I knew that he was hurting. He tried to get me to join the others, but I stayed with him. We would just walk slowly and chat about the things we saw and sit and rest every once in a while. However, when we reached a sitting area near the Matterhorn ride, Aunt Linda decided that I *had* to go on that ride. I did my best to get out of it. I cried, I begged and I cried some more, but she insisted. The attendant person at the ride said that maybe it was best if I didn't go on the ride, but Aunt Linda wouldn't take *no* for an answer. Finally, I mustered up my courage, realizing that I had no other choice than to go on this ride once and for all. "Please", I begged once more as I looked into Aunt Linda's eyes. But before she could respond, the ride took off. Each twist and turn came out a louder scream. When the ride came to a stop and the belt unlocked, I got my scarred self off, took one step and fainted. When I came to, I was in Aunt Linda's arms and she was saying how sorry she was. After that, she *never* made me go on another ride again. I stuck to watching the shows. And you know what? Come to think of it, besides the log ride and the boat ride, Aunt Linda never went on any scary rides either.

One Friday night, while Uncle Joe was on an overnight fishing trip, Aunt Linda and I were the only ones awake and we decided that we were going to stay up really late and watch *Creature Features* on channel 2. It aired on Friday nights for about 2-3 hours. We were ready! We were each in our pajamas, sitting side by side in the living room in separate recliner chairs. We had hot chocolate beside us and a big bag of popcorn between us and our blankets on top of us. We turned out all of the lights. As the credits were being shown on the tv, eerie music played for what seemed like forever. When the movie began, it started very slowly and the eerie music continued. Aunt Linda and I hid our eyes with our hands, and of course peeked through our fingers. When the music came to a sudden stop and a person or thing thrusted onto the screen, we screamed! We then hid our faces inside our blankets and argued over who was going to get up and turn the tv off, because we had no idea where the remote control was. We finally agreed to get up as fast as we could together and run to the tv and turn it off. After that, we slept together in her bed and never again turned *Creature Features* back on.

Growing up, I was pretty much marked as the goody-good girl. I didn't ever want to cause trouble for anyone or be in trouble. I hated disappointing anyone. I felt "lucky" to have a family and a home, so I always did my chores, and then some. I was a true people pleaser, I guess you could say. That caused trouble in my family because I was rarely, if ever in trouble, I would be rewarded with things. Things like a lunch date, a movie date and one time, my own cat. This upset the other kids, which caused me to stay pretty much to myself. I loved drawing, journaling and reading, so I did a lot of that. Being made fun of about my teeth, being underweight and shy really made me stay clear of others, unless they were a (safe) adult.

The six of us kids would sometimes wrestle in one of the bedrooms. Sometimes someone would hold my arms tightly together. No one had any idea why this scared me so much, but it made me feel like I couldn't breath and because of that, it seemed that my arms would be held longer and tighter. I was told that I could still breath, because my mouth was not closed. They didn't understand that my (undiagnosed) claustrophobia was para-lyzing me. After a couple of times of this happening, I chose not to wrestle with the others anymore.

Lisa was often given the job of looking after the five of us when Aunt Linda and Uncle Joe went out. Understandably, Lisa resented having to do that. She was a kid herself. There were a few times, I don't recall why, she locked Donny and I inside the jacket closet. It was a small closet with one door and the door had horizontal louvers on it from top to bottom. She propped a chair up against the doorknob. All six of us kids would be home alone. Donny and I would yell out for someone to open the door. We could see them walk by through the louver openings in the door. Fear gripped me here again, because I felt like I couldn't breathe. In my mind, I recalled the feeling of terror that I had from what both Bob and Ken had done to me. I almost blacked out when I felt that way. I would try to breathe through the openings in the door, but it was so hard. When the door was finally opened, Donny and I both collapsed onto the floor. Aunt Linda and Uncle Joe would later come home and question how everything went while they were out. We didn't dare tell. Lisa had no idea why we reacted that way. I know that she had a big responsibility of trying to take care of the five of us. She was a teenager and I am sure she had better things that she wanted to be doing.

Discipline in our house was yelling. If yelling didn't work, the belt came out. It was a black leather belt with silver medal designs on it. I witnessed all of the kids at one time or another trying to escape being hit by that belt by running from Aunt Linda while she chased them with it around the coffee table. This caused more of a rage, so I am sure the belt hurt more when they were finally caught. I was scared of that belt. I believe the fear of the belt may have been one of the reasons why

I tried so hard to stay out of trouble. There were times that one of the kids would hide the belt, but it would always be found.

The dreaded chores we had in our family were doing the dishes and doing the laundry because with a family of eight there were always lots of dishes to be washed and loads and loads of laundry to do.

During the summers, Mt. Eden High School offered swimming all day for 10 cents on Mondays. We loved that! We would pack up a lunch and take it with us. There were three swimming pools. One was for little kids and went up to two feet. The next one was 3 feet to 6 feet and was for anyone who could swim and the last pool was the high dive swimming pool, it was 11 feet deep. It had a low dive diving board and a high dive diving board. People would dive in and swim to the ladder and exit the pool. There were two lifeguards at each pool. I was scared of the water, so I mostly stayed at the three-foot mark of the second pool. We played Marco Polo in the pool and water volleyball. When it would become overcrowded, I would exit. Aunt Linda signed me up for swim lessons to help me get more comfortable with the water. When summer was almost over, I became more comfortable with the water. One year when it was two weeks before the pool was to close down, I did it! I mustered up enough courage to dive off of the low diving board. I was scared to do it, but after I did it, it felt so good. The next year, after I had jumped off of the high dive and made it across to the exit ladder, the lifeguard actually cheered for me. I was so happy when I conquered the diving board.

Chapter 6

THE DIABETES DIAGNOSIS

I n November of 1981, as I walked through the first living room, I tripped over a pedal of a bicycle and hit my right knee pretty hard on the cement floor. Overnight, it swelled up like a balloon. Aunt Linda made an appointment for me with an Orthopedic Doctor. They saw me two days later. I was told that I had water on my knee and that I would need to get it drained. I was so scared of needles. Aunt Linda knew this, because if I was ever told that I was going to have to get a shot or immunizations, she would not tell me, because I would be so scared that I wouldn't eat for days, until the appointment was over. I asked God to take the swelling away so I wouldn't have to get my knee drained. The appointment was scheduled for the following week. The day after I had first seen the Orthopedic Doctor, Ginger and I were at our friend, Carrie's house for a slumber party. That night, we went to the movies. I remember the girls handing me handfuls of candy, but I just put the candy in my pocket, because I wasn't feeling good. The night is like a fog to me. After the movie, we went back to Carrie's house and I went and laid down. Everyone thought it was because of my knee, so they let me rest. The next morning all of us girls (six of us) were at the table eating honeycomb cereal and afterwards we were going to go watch a soccer game that one of the girls sisters was going to be playing in. It took all my might to lift a spoon of cereal to my mouth and when I finally did, because I couldn't close my mouth, the honeycombs just spilled out. After my third try and after Carrie's mom saw my failed attempts at feeding myself, she decided that it would be best if I went home and skipped the game. Before driving the girls to the game, she drove me home and Ginger walked me into the house and laid me on the couch in the living room. Approximately two hours later, Ginger arrived back home and when she saw me still lying on the couch, lying in the same position that she had left me in, she tried to shake me awake, but I could only let out a faint groan. She quickly went and pounded on Aunt Linda and Uncle Joe's bedroom door and asked them if they had seen me yet that morning. When they said that they hadn't, she told them that they had to come out and look at me right then. They did and were shocked that I looked so lifeless. Aunt Linda, knowing that I loved orange julius drinks, made me one. She thought that maybe I was dehydrated and that if I drank it, maybe I would feel better. She tried to put it in my hand, but because I was so limp, I couldn't hold it. She then propped me up and tried to pour some in my mouth, but it just poured right back out of my mouth. That was when she decided that she needed to take me to the doctor. When I was seen by the doctor, they said that I would need to be taken to the Oakland Children's Hospital right away. Aunt Linda had no intention of waiting for an ambulance to take me. She carried me back to the station wagon and drove at top speed to the children's hospital. I was taken right in. They tried to get a blood sample from me, but because my blood was too thick, they had to go into my neck for a sample. I was now in a coma.

Three days later, when I woke up from the coma, I was told that I had juvenile diabetes. I had no idea what that was. They tried to explain it to me, but when I heard them say, "shots for the rest of your life," I shut down. I was 14 years old, a freshman in high school and 48 pounds. My blood sugar when I came in was exceeding the charts. They said that I was closer to death than I could realize. I thought that death sounded so much better than taking injections for the rest of my life. I had a Diabetes Specialist, Dr. Braun who came in several times a day each day and she taught me how to take care of my diabetes. I had to practice injections by injecting water into an orange. That was nothing compared to injecting myself. I also had to learn how to check the glucose (sugar) in my urine. I had three test tubes, just like you would see in a science classroom, a test tube holder, a few eyedroppers and some tablets. I had to urinate in a medical plastic cup, set the tablet in one of the test tubes, add three drops of urine and watch it foam up and turn a color. The color would indicate what my blood sugar was and how much insulin I would need to take. I took a long-acting insulin at night and a fast-acting insulin at meals.

Uncle Joe sat with me one day during one of the diabetes lessons. He rooted me on. He knew that I hadn't eaten much of anything while I was at the hospital. The nurses tried to get me to eat. I was in the pediatric department and there were kids strolling up and down the hallways. Sometimes they would be eating popsicles, ice cream cones, potato chips, juice, sodas. There was a popcorn popper machine right outside my hospital room door and the smell of freshly popped salted and buttered popcorn filled the air. I couldn't have any of the sweets and I couldn't have juice or soda. When I finally said that I would have some pop-corn, because the salt and butter smelled so good, they were glad, but said that I wouldn't be able to have salt or butter on it. How could popcorn ever taste good without salt or butter? It couldn't. To make them happy and to get them to stop asking me what I wanted to eat, when I couldn't seem to have anything at all, I decided that I would eat the very plain, tasteless and boring popcorn. Uncle Joe decided that if I took a shot then he would make sure that I would get to eat a hamburger and french fries from McDonald's. Doctor Braun said that she couldn't allow that, because of my diabetes. Uncle Joe looked her straight in the eyes and declared that if I took that shot, he was not only going to go get me a hamburger and french fries, he was also going to make sure that I not only ate it all, but that I also enjoyed every bite. She reluctantly agreed. I had been trying for three hours to get the needle into my leg. At last, I did it. I set the needle on my thigh and very slowly pushed down on it, until finally the needle was in. Then I very slowly pushed the insulin in. I did it! Was it easier the next time? No! And did I get a hamburger and french fries? Yes! In fact, I had two hamburgers and I enjoyed every bite, with Uncle Joe smiling at me the whole time. Doctor Braun apologized to Uncle Joe for being so stern. I don't know if it was reverse psychology or not, but before we left the hospital, Dr. Braun said that she expected to see me within the next few days, because I would have a hard time following through with taking care of my diabetes.

I was in the hospital for a week before I was sent home. Taking care of my diabetes was hard in many ways. I had to carry my insulin, urine supplies, and snacks with me everywhere I went. I also had to make sure that I had a sugar source with me, just in case my blood glucose dropped. Because it was hard to check my urine at school, and as you can imagine a bit embarrassing, I opted not to eat at all while I was at school. I was so glad that I didn't need to take my urine supplies with me anymore. But I did need to still make sure I had a sugar source with me, because if my glucose dropped too low, I could become unconscious. I was embarrassed to tell people about my diabetes. I didn't know anyone else who had it. I didn't want people to have something else to tease me about or maybe think that they could *catch* diabetes from me. I had to go see Dr. Braun every six months for a diabetes checkup. She was so surprised at my first six-month appointment that I had not needed to come back to her and that I didn't have any problems. (I wasn't going to let her win. I had to show her that I could manage my diabetes. Mission accomplished!)

One of the hardest things I had to learn to live with after being diagnosed with diabetes was not being able to have dessert with my family. Dessert was a nightly occurrence at our house and there weren't any sugar-free options. It was hard on Aunt Linda, too. She didn't want the other kids to miss out on dessert, but she also didn't want me to miss out. We decided that I would have fruit or (salted and buttered) popcorn. I was good with that.

Joey and Donny, being the curious boys that they were, decided one day to do experiments in the bathroom where my test tubes and urine test tablets were. They put soda, Kool Aid and even bubble solution into the test tubes with the urine tablets and watched them bubble up and splatter and make noise. This proved to be a very expensive experiment. Aunt Linda made the decision that all of my supplies would now be stored in her bedroom bathroom and I would do my testing in there. None of the kids liked that idea because no one was ever allowed in Aunt Linda and Uncle Joe's room until now.

Our family spent a lot of time at Rocky's Pizza on Mission Boulevard in Hayward. Lisa and Tony's first step dad (an earlier relationship that Aunt Linda had been involved in), Louie, owned it. We loved it there. We played billiards, listened to the jukebox, learned how to make pizza and we all often worked there making pizzas and cleaning up the pizza parlor at the end of the night. One night, after closing, Tony and I were restocking the shelves and as I was checking the walk-in freezer to make sure the stock was good, the door latched shut behind me. Thankfully, Tony was close by and he had seen what happened and he was able to open the door promptly. Whew!

Both my mom and my grandma were buried in a cemetery right down the street from Rocky's Pizza. I often took my lunch there and sat on the grass and went through my memories that were stored in my heart. It was soothing.

The summer before I started my freshman year, our family went on a camping trip to Woodward Reservoir in Oakdale, California. It was really hot there! We were used to the Bay Area weather, high's in the 70's. We were camping in 101 degree weather. We stayed in the water to keep cool. Because I am so fair skinned, when I decided to take a nap on my stomach on a raft in the middle of the lake for two hours, you could imagine how burned my backside became. When I woke up, I paddled myself onto the shore with my hands, not realizing how burned I was. When I lifted myself out of the water and carried the raft behind me, I let out a yelp. The raft had rubbed up against the back of my thighs. When I looked at the back of my legs, they were bright red and blistered. I had succeeded in barbecuing a Patty–me! I couldn't sit, lay down and I could barely walk for about a week. One evening, after returning home from the camping trip Ginger and I walked to our friend, Carrie's house. Carrie and other friends were meeting us halfway. When they turned the corner I heard them asking each other, "Why is she wearing shorts? She is so white." When I turned around, they understood why. I had first and second degree burns down the back of my legs.

Chapter 7

WE'RE MOVING?

It was my sophomore year, I was 15 years old and it was the month of December. We had a family meeting and it was announced that we would be moving. We were all shocked and asked why we were moving, where would we be moving to and when we would be moving. We were told that by February we would be moving to a place called Ceres, California. We had never heard of Ceres, California. We were also told that Ceres was an hour and a half from where we were currently living. I was devastated. This would mean changing schools, leaving my church and my friends and everything I was comfortable with. I tried to boycott going. Of course, it didn't work. During this time a custody battle began between Uncle Joe and Ginger and Joey's mom. Ginger and Joey didn't want to move, and after much conversing, it was decided that they would stay in

Hayward, with their mom and her husband. After this, I didn't see Ginger and Joey very often.

We indeed did move to Ceres, California in early February. When we arrived at the house because it was not yet vacant, we stayed in a hotel in a nearby town. On our first night of the three nights that we were at the hotel, we went to a Roller King skating rink. It was a lot of fun. A lot of teens were there and there was loud music and bright strobe lights. The next night, we discovered cruising on McHenry Blvd.

When we moved into the house in Ceres, it was a nice house and it was across the street from a park that had tennis courts. I started Ceres High School right away. Another school, in the middle of the school year. I pretty much stayed to myself. The high school was a little over a mile from our house. Each morning on my walk to school, I talked to God and recalled songs and Bible verses that I had been taught and the Christian songs that I knew. My family had not attempted to find a church, and I didn't want to find one alone, so this is how I thought I would have church. It was lonely though. I missed the singing, the people and the Bible learning.

Aunt Linda opened a home cleaning business called Linda's Quick and Clean. She was passionate about it. This business caused there to be a lot of foot traffic in our house, but we were already used to that. Uncle Joe was still working on friend's cars to make extra money. Another thing he was doing was growing and selling marijuana. This scared me. They openly smoked it and even smoked it with Lisa. They thought that it was better if she smoked it with them rather than smoke it behind their backs. She drank with them, too. It bothered me, but what could I say to them about it? There was a story that had been on the news about a family that was growing marijuana in their backyard. Because of that, their child was taken away from them. I thought that could happen to Donny and I. I'm not at all proud of what I did, but I decided that I had to get rid of it, so I gave it away. And it wasn't any trouble at all. I seemed to have a lot of friends after that. When I realized that what I was doing was not helping anything, I stopped. I was talked into trying marijuana once, but after one puff, I knew I didn't like it. Also, I thought it was embarrassing how people acted after they had smoked it. I didn't want to even try drinking. I saw the rages that came from people who had drunk alcohol. I also saw how people would not have any memory of what they did or said after they woke up from passing out, and the headaches that they would get. None of that looked appealing to me.

I don't know why, but I resented at times being called a goody-good girl. Maybe because when people said it, they did so in an accusing way. One day I decided that I was going to buy cigarettes. Not just any type of cigarettes, they would have to be pretty ones, if they existed. I chose Virginia Slims, because they had a satin look to them. I never smoked them, I just thought that having them sitting in my purse might have everyone stop calling me a goody-good-girl. After a while, I thought that I better scuff up the tips to make them look like they had been smoked and throw some away, I couldn't have a full pack of cigarettes in my purse every day. One night, after skating at the Roller King, Tony was sent to pick up my friends and I. After Tony dropped off my friends at their homes, Tony let me know that he had seen me smoking. He was shocked. I couldn't take it. I showed him the pretty unsmoked Virginia Slims and he laughed and laughed. "Why buy them if you are not going to smoke them?" he asked. I told him that I was tired of being called a goody-good-girl so I thought I would carry cigarettes. He laughed again and said, "Well that only proves what everyone is saying–you are a goody-good-girl." He never told Aunt Linda and Uncle Joe.

After Lisa turned 18, she moved out on her own, with roommates due to there being a lot of friction between her and both Aunt Linda and Uncle Joe. She moved to Castro Valley.

Tony and I were close. He and Lisa were part Puerto Rican and looking at Tony, you could tell.

He had beautiful brown skin and very curly afro-type hair. One family trip we went on was to Mexico. On our way back, we had to stop at the border so they could make sure we weren't smuggling anything or anyone out of Mexico. Well, because Tony was much darker than any of the rest of us and because his hair was afro-type curly, they thought that we were smuggling Tony out of Mexico. It took a couple of hours, but thankfully Tony made it back home with us.

Tony had a way of pretty much talking me into almost anything. The main thing he talked me into was making him huge *Patti-specials*, he would call them. That was a sandwich with everything on it, wrapped tightly in a paper towel. He would grin the whole time he ate it. He could have made it himself, he would tell me, "but everything always tastes better when someone else makes it." (I fell for that all the way up until he moved out.) Tony moved out when he was 19 years old. He also made his way back to the Bay Area and moved in with Louie. Because their birth dad had not been in their lives from early on, Lisa and Tony considered Louie to be their dad.

It was odd when the only kids in the house were Donny and I. We actually had our own bedrooms. I enjoyed decorating my room in my own way. Another nice thing about having my own room was if I wanted to be by myself, no one would barge in.

I loved drawing and writing. I would doodle on just about anything. I later learned that my dad enjoyed drawing and found it a way to relax.

Donny seemed to be more and more to himself when we moved to Ceres. He would close himself in his room a lot and listen to loud music.

I still had my braces and still had my dreaded neck gear that I was to wear at night, but on my own I stopped wearing it every night and went to every other night, because my jaw was aching a lot. At times my jaw would lock open and when it did that, it hurt. Aunt Linda was not happy that I wasn't wearing it every night. She thought that I wasn't wearing it because I just didn't want to. And when I tried to explain my reasons for not wanting to wear it, I was given what I had never gotten before or since then, a slap across the face. I am not sure what hurt more, my face or my feelings. I grabbed my cheek and scurried to my room. The next day she made an appointment with an orthodontist, Dr. Mettler. The next week we went in for the appointment. After he did the x-rays, he came in and told Aunt Linda that he was very sorry for the care that I had been given. When she questioned him more, he explained that I had most likely been done with my braces treatment for up to a year and a half and wearing the neck gear was causing wear on my jaw. He asked me if my jaw had been aching or popping. Teary eyed, I said, "Yes." Aunt Linda put her hand on my hand and said that she was so sorry for being mad at me over this. She was upset that she didn't get this checked out more thoroughly in Hayward. Dr. Mettler said that he wanted to take my braces off and finish my orthodontic care at no cost to us. Aunt Linda could not accept that from him. She offered to repay him by having her cleaning business clean his office until all of the cost that my care would entail was paid off. He was adamant that he could not allow that and wanted to give us the care we had already paid for in Hayward, but didn't get. His generosity was graciously accepted.

After my braces were removed our family went out to dinner, just as my grandma had wanted us to do and I loved my new smile.

In early 1984, I was so glad when I was told by my Endocrinologist (Diabetes Dr.) that I wouldn't have to take urine tests anymore. Instead, I would be taking glucose (blood) tests, but this meant more needles. Five or six times a day I would need to check my glucose. I was given an Accu-Chek machine. It was beige in color and was about 12 inches long by 5 inches wide. It had a place to put my glucose strip and I had a hammer like needle pricker. It took hours for me to poke my finger for the first few times or more. The machine took two minutes to test and the bell on it that rang when the result was ready was very loud. It drew attention every time I used it. But it was far better than doing urine tests.

After Aunt Tina married Uncle Ron, they had Jenny. Donny and I became very close to Jenny because Aunt Tina and Uncle Ron would at times have us over on weekends. When Jenny was a toddler, Aunt Tina had a home daycare and she would let me come over during the summers and help her. They lived in Livermore, California. I loved helping her with the kids in the daycare. I already knew that I one day wanted to be a teacher, but now I thought that preschoolers would be fun. Aunt Tina and Uncle Ron were fun to be with. We spent a lot of time swimming at a community pool nearby. Uncle Ron loved to swim and he was really good at it. He had once been a lifeguard. Uncle Ron was also a prankster. One evening Auntie and I went on a walk with Jenny in the stroller. We were in deep conversation and as we turned the corner, toward their house we heard something in the bushes. Thinking it was a cat, I stooped down and suddenly out of the bushes came Uncle Ron with a loud scream. He was dressed in a ninja costume. He scared the daylights out of Jenny and Auntie and I. He sure did get a great laugh out of it though. There were many neighborhood water fights at their house. Uncle Ron did the extreme. He would hide in the house and then put a hose up to the kitchen sink and spray us from the window.

I spent a lot of time sitting in the front yard of Aunt Tina and Uncle Ron's house. Lavonne and Dick lived across the street and they had three sons. I sat outside in hopes that one of their boys would come over and talk. They didn't. We all became friends. I just happened to notice them more than they noticed me.

I spent three wonderful summers with Auntie. She and Uncle Ron were great positive role models. They had a strong marriage. They communicated with each other. They were honest with each other. They had fun together. They enjoyed each other's company. They had what I one day wanted for myself, but didn't really believe was possible, a relationship of true love and devotion.

It was at Aunt Tina and Uncle Ron's house when I discovered I had the dreadful chicken pox. It was 100 degrees and I was covered in them. Auntie took care of me. Another time during my time there I sprained my arm. There were a few times that I had insulin reactions. One time, while we were grocery shopping, I became tongue tied, distant and sweaty. Auntie kept asking me if something was wrong. I kept telling her that there wasn't anything wrong, but my body was saying the opposite. She took a candy bar from a shelf on the candy aisle, opened it and told me to eat it. I told her that I couldn't. She forcibly told me to eat it again. Pushing the candy bar away, I said that I didn't want it. Finally, because my energy was gone and my body was going limp, I ate the candy bar. My brain was telling me that I had not bought the candy bar, so I couldn't eat it. Aunt Tina told me that when we reached the checkout counter we would tell them what happened and pay for the candy bar. When a Type 1 diabetic has low blood sugar, it is odd how they can recall laws, but can't get their brain around taking care of their insulin reaction with a simple drink of juice or a food item containing sugar.

One summer, while at Aunt Tina and Uncle Ron's house, I caught a flu bug. My body still needed insulin, but because I couldn't keep any food down, my blood sugar dropped way down. Auntie took me to the hospital and I was given a dextrose injection. I was also given an I.V. Auntie didn't like the sight of blood no better than I did. When the doctor took the I.V. from the vein in my wrist, he sternly told her to press firmly onto my wrist, right where the needle had been for approximately three minutes. He told her not to move or lift her fingers from my wrist. If she did, we were told that blood would splatter out from my wrist. We knew that we couldn't let that happen. Auntie held onto my wrist with all of her might.

Because it seemed the only time I ever got sick was when I was at Auntie's house, when she would invite me over for a weekend or longer, she would jokingly ask me to please not get sick.

Aunt Linda and Joe had problems with trust and because of that, they felt that they couldn't trust the people around them either, even their kids. The mistrust put wedges between them and Lisa, Tony and Donny, causing them all to move out of the house rather quickly after turning 18. Donny though moved in with Aunt Tina and Uncle Ron during his high school years and finished high school in Livermore.

Due to how dreadfully thin I was, I decided to wear layers of clothes under my clothes. It would be leg warmers, sweats, thermals–anything that would make me look less thin. I also wore baggy shirts, two at a time. I hated being teased and that seemed to be an easy fix. I was always cold, so the thick layers weren't too uncomfortable for me. Most people think that only heavy people get made fun of. That's not at all true. Anyone and everyone can be made fun of. People who are tall, short, heavy, thin, acne, no acne, busty, not busty, braces, glasses, freckles, shyness, ethnicity, popularity, loner, rich, poor. It is endless how many different things that people can be teased for. And each of those circumstances can really scar someone for a lifetime. I wish that there was a way to put an end to teasing.

Chapter 8

THE BLIND DATE THAT WOULD CHANGE MY LIFE

I t was the first day back at school in September of 1984. I had just returned the day before from a summer with Aunt Tina and Uncle Ron. It was the beginning of my Senior year of high school. As I was getting my schedule of classes for the new school year, my friend Tonja came up to me and asked me if I had a boyfriend. When I told her that I did not, she exclaimed, "Don't look at anyone, talk to anyone, or give anyone your number. I have the perfect guy for you!" "The perfect guy?" I thought. You see, Tonja had a rough life and the people she knew were rough. I was a bit scared. She told me that she had given a guy named Tim my phone number. I couldn't believe that she gave my phone number out to a guy that I didn't even know. She smiled a huge smile and proclaimed that I was really going to like him. She went on to tell me that

Tim was her boyfriend's roommate. I hadn't even met her boyfriend.

That night Tim called me. At first, it was awkward. I found it hard to talk to someone that I didn't know. He also thought it was awkward. I was 16 years old, he was 21. He had already had trouble with the age gap, but when he heard my small voice on the telephone he thought, "Oh no, she's not even 16, she's 14." After talking for about an hour, we decided that we would go on a double date with Tonja and her boyfriend Todd on that Saturday night. Boy was I nervous. I was being set up. I was trusting Tonja. I did a lot of praying. I asked God to keep me safe and for Him to help me not be so nervous. Aunt Linda and Uncle Joe were okay with the double dating idea. They were cautious though. Earlier that year, I had had a bad relationship with someone who was a couple of years older than me and when I refused to allow him to go further than I wanted, he bashed the back of my head into the outside of a car passenger door. Uncle Joe was furious when I came into the house crying. Before the guy turned around and drove off, Uncle Joe hurried out and confronted him, giving him his two-cents! Another time, a guy that I was getting close to called me and told me that he was ill and needed some Tylenol. but he didn't have any. He asked me if I could bring him some. He was just down the street therefore I didn't see any problem with it. When I arrived at his house, he was in the back bedroom. He called me back. I cautiously went down the hall, prepared to throw the sandwich baggie that had 6 Tylenol for him on the bed that I thought he would be laying on. Instead, he was at the bedroom door. When he saw me, he took my arm and pulled me into the bedroom, closing the door behind me. When I asked him what he was doing, he told me that he thought that us being together would help him feel better and he grabbed my other arm and tried to pull me toward him. I pushed him away and told him that I was leaving. He laughed and told me not to leave, but to get ready for some fun. I raised my voice at him and declared that I was leaving. When I was finally able to pull my arms from him, I opened the bedroom door, but he grabbed me and pulled me back in. I then kicked him in his groin and when he bent down in pain, I ran home. Again, Uncle Joe was furious when I ran in and told him and Aunt Linda about what had happened. Uncle Joe went into the garage and then he went out to his truck that was parked in the driveway and sped off down the street. He never told me what happened or what words were exchanged between him and the guy that I had told him about. Thankfully, I never saw that guy again. You can now see why I was so nervous and why Aunt Linda and Uncle Joe were so cautious. Uncle Joe and

Aunt Linda always had my best interest in mind. They were protective over me, just like parents should be over their kids.

When Tonja and I drove up to the triplex that Tim and Todd shared together, Tim and Todd were playing darts in the garage and an extra-large Rico's pizza was waiting to be eaten. After Tonja introduced me, both Tim and I were filled with nervousness. Tim seemed very uncomfortable. That made me feel even more nervous. We all made small talk and ate some pizza. About two hours later, we went to a billiards pool hall and played pool. Tonja rode with Todd and I rode with Tim in his yellow courier pickup truck. We were now getting more comfortable with talking to each other. We had a good time at the pool hall. On the way back to Tim and Todd's house, while we were stopped at a red light, he asked me if he could kiss me. I felt my face turn so many shades of pink and as my heart fluttered, I told him that he could. As he cupped my chin in his palm, he kissed me softly on my lips. That kiss took my breath away. I was so touched that he actually *asked* me for a kiss. He never forced himself on me. He was kind and considerate of my feelings. We stayed out for hours. I spent that night at Tonja's house. She wanted to know how I felt about Tim. I told her that I thought he was really nice. She said, "Good, then we are going to do it again next week." She was up to something, that's for sure, and I didn't mind at all.

The next day, when I came home from Tonja's house, Aunt Linda and Uncle Joe were curious about the date. I let them know that I had a nice time and that I thought that they would like Tim. They wanted to make sure that Tim did not over-step his boundaries and were pleasantly surprised when I told them that he actually asked me for a kiss (points earned!). They still however were not happy with him being 21. They had many reser-vations about it, but said they would think about it more, if I should even think about dating him. To me, there was nothing to think about. I was already falling for him, big time!

Tim called me the next evening. We talked and learned more about each other. He worked as a jeweler repairing jewelry. He had a Monday through Friday job and great hours, 7-4:30. He was an Air Force Brat and had four siblings. Three were older and one was younger. He was also close to his mom and dad who lived in a nearby town. I gave him just a few details about me. I lived with my Aunt and Uncle because my mom had died, I had 5 'siblings', I had diabetes and I loved animals. I thought that was enough for now. We talked again on Monday and he asked if he could maybe come over on Tuesday to meet Aunt Linda and Uncle Joe. I told him that I would ask them to see if they were up to it. When I talked to them about it, they were a bit wary, but agreed to have him over. I was so nervous about it. What if they didn't like him? What if he didn't like them? What if after he met them, he didn't want to go out with me again? I was on pins and needles.

Tim would tell you that he was born with a birth defect. The birth defect is being late for everything! He was supposed to be at my house at 7 that evening, but arrived at 7:20. I thought maybe he had chickened out of coming over. He was nervous when he knocked on the door. After he was invited in, Aunt Linda and Uncle Joe asked him quite a few questions. Then Aunt Linda said that she had something to tell him. "Oh No!" I thought. "What is she going to say to him?" I was not prepared for this at all. She looked straight at him and said, "We are not thrilled with the age gap between you and Patti. She has had bad experiences with older guys before. I want you to know that if you are going to date a 16-year-old then you are going to have to live by a 16-year-old's rules." He said that he didn't have a problem with that. Aunt Linda then told him that phone calls would be at a 15-minute limit (part of the reason for that was because of her cleaning business), we could only see each other two times during the work/school week and no calls or visits past 9:00 pm. But we could still go out on Friday or Saturday night's. He agreed to all of that. (Points achieved).

Our visits were mostly on Tuesdays and Thursdays. We lived across the street from a park therefore I would usually wait for him at the park, while walking Brandy and Scruffy, our two dogs that we had during that time. He would try to be there by 7, but still always made it by 7:20. This flustered me, because 9:00 seemed to come pretty fast. Tim shared more about himself with me. He shared that about 4 months prior to us meeting, he had been engaged to someone and had called it off three days before they were to be married. I was surprised at that. When I asked him why they had called it off, he said that he realized that he wanted to be married, but not to that person. He also told me that the year before that he had been in a bad car accident. He had been drinking and had been out with friends and on the way home, he fell asleep and crashed into a ditch that was across from a cemetery and below a set of railroad tracks. It was in the middle of the night in October and it was pretty chilly. The battery flew out of his truck and he was trapped inside. When he came to, he told me that he didn't know if he had crashed into anyone or not. He had cracked ribs and he had a broken leg. He called out for help, but no one heard him. He was trapped for more than 5 hours before two young boys riding bicycles through the area heard his calls for help. Also, a train conductor saw him when they passed by him in the early morning and called 911. He was in the hospital for one month. When he recalls this story, he talks about his dire need for Chapstick during those hours he was trapped. When the ambulance came and tended to him and asked him if he needed anything, "Chapstick," was his reply. They didn't have any. When he arrived at the hospital he again asked for Chapstick, but still none was found. His sister eventually brought him his much needed Chapstick. He said that since then, he has made sure that he has Chapstick with him wherever he goes. Tim also shared that he used alcohol to help cure his shyness. He had not planned on the alcohol getting out of hand, and causing an accident that could have possibly taken the life of someone else. This was on his mind a lot.

When I shared with Tim that I was a Christian, he didn't mind at all. In fact, he said that he had grown up going to Sunday School and at times watched the 700 Club and the PTL (Praise the Lord) program with his mom. He wondered if I went to church. I told him that I didn't, because I had no one to go with. He then told me that he had been praying that God would send him a girl that would lead him to Jesus. This made my heart smile. We talked about going to church and he talked to his older brother, Rick and his wife Lynn who were Christians about it.

On his lunch hour, Tim would often pick me up at my lunch time at Ceres High School. We would park in a church parking lot and talk. One day during this time, he said to me, "What we have is a gift from God. If we want to keep what we have, we need to get our lives right with God." I was in full agreement. He then said, "We just have to find a church to go to." "Why not here?" I said. We were in the parking lot of a downtown church called Ceres Christian Church. He thought that was a good idea. The next Sunday we went to church. I loved it.

Tim asked me to be his girlfriend on September 21, 1984. On my birthday, November 20, just a little over two months after we had met, Tim gave me a beautiful gold, diamond and topaz, (my birth-stone) promise ring. He had it wrapped in a pampers diaper box because he joked, "I am robbing the cradle." I accepted it. Aunt Linda and Joe were surprised about this and they still had their rules for Tim and I to follow.

Aunt Linda's employees always arrived very early in the mornings, she woke up at 4 am One early morning she heard something outside. The dogs were barking ferociously. Uncle Joe got out one of his guns and when they looked out the window, they saw a yellow truck drive off. They heard something in the wind. When they went out-side, they found balloons tied to the mailbox and flowers were hanging out of the mailbox with a note for me, from Tim. He did this countless times, but he was also very smart about it because at times he included something for Aunt Linda. (More points scored!) The balloons had sentimental mes-sages. Messages like "I Love You," and "Thinking of You" They were all heart shaped.

Even though I had told Tim about my diabetes, he didn't know anything about the autoimmune disease. One Saturday, Aunt Linda and Uncle Joe were gone for the day and Tim came over for a good part of the day. We were watching a movie on tv when I had an insulin reaction. For some odd reason, I was embarrassed to eat in front of Tim, therefore when my blood sugar dropped, I didn't get up to do anything about it, which was a very bad idea! I was very quiet and distant. Tim had the impression that I was going to break up with him. When he got up to leave, I pulled his arm back and asked him to sit down and I went to get a glass of orange juice. That was the first time he had witnessed an insulin reaction, but not the last. The next day, he decided that we were going to go to a fast food restaurant and eat together so that is what we did. He also decided that he wanted to learn all that he could about my diabetes. He asked Aunt Linda if he could go with us the next time we went to Oakland for my diabetes appointment. She agreed to it and at my next appointment, Tim asked Dr. Braun a lot of questions, which impressed both her and Aunt Linda. It also made me more comfortable. I had earlier thought that if he knew about the ups and downs of diabetes that he would get scared about it and would not want to be in a relationship with me. Thankfully, I was wrong! He told me that there were three things that he had prayed to God for before we met. 1) That God would send him a girl that would lead him to Jesus. 2) She would love everyone and everything and 3) She would have some kind of physical ailment so that he could prove to her how much he loved her, in spite of that physical ailment and he added a P.S… he wanted the girl to be thin because he had a *thing* for thin girls. He said that he thought that God had answered his prayers on all three counts, and even the P.S. Him telling me this really humbled me. I realized that God had gifted me with my true love.

Even while dating, I still wore layers. Tim even commented on it. I told him that I wore layers because I had a skin condition, but that wasn't the reason for the layers. I was just so thin and I was embarrassed by it. In time, Tim made me feel more comfortable with my thinness and I stopped wearing layers. I also still carried those pretty Virginia Slim cigarettes. He asked me if I would stop smoking. I explained to him that I had no trouble stopping because I didn't really smoke. He challenged me to throw them away and I did. A few days later he wondered if I missed smoking or if I craved a cigarette. I told him that I didn't miss it, nor did I crave it at all. He saw that what I had said was true and he said that he had never recalled my breath ever smelling like smoke or my lips tasting like smoke when he kissed me. My clothes always smelled like smoke because Aunt Linda and Uncle Joe smoked.

Tim decided that he wanted to know about me in great detail. He wondered about my dad. I knew that my dad was remarried to a woman named Bonnie and they had a son named Tom. My dad had told Bonnie about me and she wrote to me a few times. One year on Father's Day, while I was at Aunt Tina's house, I mustered up the courage to call my dad to wish him a Happy Father's Day. He was shocked that I called and said that he thought it would be best if I didn't call him. I was crushed. I felt like he was rejecting me therefore I said goodbye and left it at that. Tom and I wrote to each other a few times, but that was the extent of it. When I told Tim about this, he decided that he would start praying that God would one day reunite me with my dad.

Tim asked me if my mom ever remarried and how she died. I told him that her choice in men was not good and that she did remarry and she died from cancer. I didn't go into great detail about anything and in time, I had blocked out of my mind a lot of what had happened to me. Maybe it was because when I would try to talk about it when I was growing up, the subject was always dismissed and I was often told that when you grow up and remember things that had happened when you were little, those things that you remember seem to be much bigger or darker than what really happened. So, I wondered, to myself, "Did I just *think* that all that happened?"

One Saturday, while Tim and I were running some errands, he drove us up to a house that I had never seen before. When I asked him where we were, he told me that we were at his parent's house. He could have told me this before we arrived there but he said that he thought I wouldn't want to go with him there. He was smart. I would have most likely made up some excuse. I sure did feel awkward. By the looks on their faces, they didn't expect to meet me either. They were nice. Ann was tall and slender with short blondish/grey hair. She was polite as she asked me questions about myself. Richard was a bit hefty in his build and had balding brown hair. He was friendly and seemed to enjoy telling jokes. Ann worked for Storer Bus Transportation. She transported kids to and from school who had special needs. Richard worked for the US Post Office as a mail handler. They made me feel welcome, but I was glad when it was time for us to go.

Tim wondered why I did not yet have a driver's learners permit or even a driver's license, since I was 16 years old. I had taken driver's training in high school, but chose not to drive. He had a hard time with that line of thinking. When I was 17, he decided that he was going to teach me how to drive, He taught me in his Ford Courier, which was a stick shift. He said that he never wanted me to be in a situation that I couldn't get out of. If I needed to get out of where I was and the only vehicle that would be around was a stick shift, then he wanted to be sure that I would still be able to get away. I didn't enjoy learning how to drive the stick shift, but I am glad that I did! I tried to take the driving test in the stick shift, but because I wasn't quite ready and Tim forgot to tell me a few small things from his earlier driver's training classes, like the hand motions, I failed. A few weeks later, after Tim was sure that he covered everything, he had me take the test in his 1973 Plymouth Duster that was an automatic. I passed.

When it was Prom time my Senior year, I had anticipated going, but Tim thought he was too old to accompany me therefore I didn't go. I understood, well sort of. I still at times give him a hard time about it. Instead of going to the Prom, he took me out to a nice dinner. I graduated high school in June of 1985, at 17 years old. Tim and I were growing closer, however Todd and Tonja were not together anymore.

Aunt Linda and Uncle Joe went to a cabin with friends a few times every year, a couple of times Tim and I accompanied them there. We barbecued together, played pool, ping-pong and went boating out on the lake. We always enjoyed doing this.

A couple of months after high school, on a Saturday night, Tim and I were at his house relaxing and watching tv when he began asking me questions. Questions like how long he thought I would want to wait before I gave any thought to marriage. He thought that maybe I would want to experience being out of high school and being on my own for a time. I told him that that was not what I planned on doing. I told him that I couldn't ever picture my life without him. A few minutes later he told me that we had to leave. I knew that I didn't have to be home for another hour or so, but I followed him. We got into his truck and he drove down the street and around the corner to where an elementary school was located. As we parked in the street next to the curb, he asked me if I would marry him. Of course, I said yes! He explained that because he wasn't sure of what my answer would be he didn't have a ring yet. That didn't matter to me. After all, I had his heart. Tim also explained that he didn't want to ask me to marry him at his house because Aunt Linda and Uncle Joe didn't know that that is where we were. Not that we were doing anything wrong while we were there, but he just thought they would understand better if they knew that he had asked me at a different location. He had already totally won over Aunt Linda and Uncle Joe by this time. They adored him! They knew he was a good person. After he dropped me off at home that night, I was so happy! I couldn't wait to tell everyone, but Tim asked me to not say anything, because he wanted to ask Aunt Linda and Uncle Joe for their permission to marry me. How was I ever going to be able to keep it to myself? The next morning, Tim picked me up for church. When we arrived at church I wanted to tell everyone, but decided not to, because for one, I didn't have a ring yet and two, Aunt Linda and Uncle Joe hadn't given us their blessing yet.

Ceres Christian Church had become an important part of our lives. We were in a Growth Group Bible Study and had been growing together in our walk with Christ. Tim was baptized a few months after we started church. Because of his shyness, he decided to be baptized at an evening service because less people went to the evening service time than the morning one. He had also stopped drinking. He was now depending on God to help him with his shyness, instead of alcohol.

When we arrived back at my house after church, Tim was a nervous wreck. Uncle Joe was watching car races on tv in the living room, Aunt Linda was in the kitchen preparing something to eat and Donny was sitting at the dining room table. Tim and I went to the kitchen and as we started to open the conversation, the telephone rang. It rang one time. We knew that it was Auntie Verla. We knew what this meant. Aunt Linda would have to call her back right then or Auntie Verla would think something was wrong and keep calling. As usual, they talked for about 45 minutes. A grueling 45 minutes of waiting it was! When the phone was hung up, we were ready! That's when two of her Quick and Clean employees came over to restock their supplies for the next morning. Aunt Linda had great relationships with her staff. When any of them came over, as you can guess, they stayed for quite a while and would sometimes even stay for lunch. Thankfully this day, they didn't stay for lunch. After they left, I called out, "Hold on! Before the phone rings or someone else comes over, we *need* to talk to both of you." That got not only their attention, but Donny's attention as well. Uncle Joe walked to the kitchen area and stood next to Aunt Linda. Donny repositioned himself in the chair he was sitting on at the dining room table. Tim took a deep breath and told them how much he loved me and how thankful he was to have me in his life. He said that he appreciated them and thanked them for opening their door and their hearts to him. It looked as though they could see what was coming. Uncle Joe heckled Tim a bit, he loved to do that every once in a while. Finally, Tim nervously said, "I would like your permission to marry Patti." Because Tim's voice was so shaky, Donny was busting up laughing. Aunt Linda started crying and Uncle Joe shed a tear as they both gave us their blessing. They hugged us and asked us when we wanted to get married. We hadn't thought of a date yet. The next day, Tim presented me with an engagement ring. I couldn't believe that I was engaged. I was on cloud 9. The following Sunday when we went to church, I couldn't wait to tell everyone that we were engaged. I was surprised though, when they told us that they thought that we were already married.

On Halloween 1985, Aunt Tina and Uncle Ron invited us to their Halloween party. Tim and I were not into Halloween, but we thought that we would go and just have fun with our family. Tim dressed up as a punk rocker and I was dressed up as a cat. Uncle Ron always had the best costumes! He worked hard on his costume that year. It was made out of thick rope. He was Cousin It from

The Addams Family. Auntie was very pregnant and was dressed as a hula girl. She was hilarious. There were a lot of people and there was alcohol. We kept our distance. After being there a while, Uncle Ron knew that I liked ice tea and he offered me some and I eagerly accepted it. Aunt Tina was close by when she heard Tim talk to me about needing a haircut. She said that she knew how to cut hair and she could cut it right then. He believed her and we went down the hall to her bedroom. She cut the left side of his hair and it looked nice, but she was a bit too tipsy to finish and cut the right side. I couldn't let Tim go back out to where the party was with just one side of his hair cut so I offered to cut the other side for him. He had long bangs and he had them pushed down onto his forehead and hair sprayed. Thankfully, I was able to match the right side with the left side. But now Tim had a completely different hairstyle on him. He was not at all happy about it, but I really liked it. During the night, I had two more refills of the ice tea and soon after, I had a horrible headache. The room was spinning, the voices in the room were echoing. I wondered what was happening to me? I was then told by my dear Uncle Ron that the ice tea that he had given me had a name. It was Long Island Iced Tea, a tea with many different alcohols. I had never drank before and what I thought I had been drinking truly did taste like ice tea, a fruity type of ice tea. I couldn't believe that I was...drunk! That was the first and only time I had ever been drunk. On the way home, because there was not yet a seat belt law, I sat on the floor of the truck with my face on the seat as I held a plastic bag to catch my vomit. All I thought about was, how could I go to church the next morning feeling like that? At 2 am, I knew that I wasn't going to be feeling well enough to go to church. Not only was I drunk, I had a hangover. What was Aunt Linda going to say? Then I remembered that I didn't know that I was drinking alcohol, Uncle Ron did. After this ordeal, I knew that drinking was not for me! How could people willingly do this to themselves? And there was no way that I would ever not want to know what I was doing the night before. And the hang-over headaches, did people really want those? I also started taking my own non alcoholic drinks with me wherever I would go.

Planning our wedding had its ups and downs! The colors we chose were mauve and gray. As a gift someone offered to make our wedding cake. Another person offered to be our photographer. We knew that we wanted a church wedding and we wanted our Pastor, Tom Salter to be the one to unite us in marriage. Because Aunt Linda and

Uncle Joe were paying for the wedding, they felt like they could make some decisions themselves. Decisions like having alcohol at the reception and having our reception in the basement of a bar. We knew that we didn't like that idea and when we told Aunt Linda that, she decided that since she had already paid for the reception, if we weren't happy with it, then *we* would need to go and get the money back and find a reception place ourselves. We decided that we would at least go take a look at the *reception* place for ourselves. After looking at the place, our decision was made. No way would we be having our wedding reception there! There were half dressed women painted on the walls and the scent of cigarettes and alcohol was in the air. Tim asked for the money back and cancelled the reservation. A few days later we were able to reserve the YMCA for our reception, and it was less expensive. Now, what were we going to do about alcohol being there? We argued with them over this. She agreed that we could do our toast with apple cider and that everyone would also use the apple cider for the toast, but after that the alcohol would be available. What could I say? We decided that we would pray about the alcohol and ask God to take care of it.

We took some time to think about how and what we were going to live on. It was apparent that we would both need to work. I didn't mind. I started looking for a job and came across a preschool that was looking for a teacher. I doubted that I would get it, because I didn't yet have any college child development units. I called them, went in to talk to them and was hired. I was now an employee at Kiddie Kollege of Nursery Knowledge. It was a house that had been remodeled into a preschool. The Director, Mrs. Jones lived with her husband next door. She was in her 80's. She was a spit-fire woman! She was a bit heavy set, hunched over slightly, had dark brown short hair with red-dish highlights. She walked with a cane and she had a gruff voice. When she hired me, she told me that if I ever decided to go to school or have kids, I would no longer have a job. Mrs. Jones' husband was a kind and gentle person. He was slender and enjoyed his walk from their house to the preschool several times throughout each day. The children loved it when Mr. Jones would come in and greet them. I always wondered what the story was with Mr. and Mrs. Jones.

During the time that I worked at Kiddie Kollege, Tim and I were married. We were married at Ceres Christian Church on July 26, 1986. I wore Aunt Tina's wedding dress. We had a small wedding. Aunt Linda and Uncle Joe had not been getting along and two nights before the wedding, I was devastated when I was told that Uncle Joe might not be going to the wedding. He was supposed to walk me down the aisle. After many tears, I asked Uncle Mike if he would mind walking me down the aisle, if Uncle Joe didn't. He said he would. Thankfully, Aunt Linda and Uncle Joe set their differences aside and Uncle Joe walked me down the aisle. And God answered our prayers about the alcohol. Only a limited amount was consumed, leaving approximately all of the three cases untouched.

I worked at Kiddie Kollege of Nursery Knowledge for a year and a half. I worked with three women, Dorothy, Darla and Lois. During the day, I was a teacher's aide and during the afternoon, I cleaned the preschool. One day while I was cleaning the preschool, Mrs. Jones made a comment that the can of soup that Darla had opened in the classroom earlier that morning belonged to the preschool and that she should have not taken it. I mentioned to Mrs. Jones that I had been with Darla the night before when she bought that particular can of soup. This did not make Mrs. Jones happy. In fact, she told me that it was none of my business and that I was done and could leave. When I told her that I still had one more room to tend to, she firmly told me that I didn't have to worry about *that* room or any other room because my work there was over. I didn't understand. As I gathered my things to leave, I looked at Mrs. Jones while she sat at her desk and asked, "My job is over?"

"You don't have to worry about coming back," she said. I was crushed when I left. I wondered what I was going to tell Tim? Had I been fired? All I did was explain that I was with Darla when she bought the can of soup. When I arrived at home, I sat on the floor and cried. I felt defeated. Tim came home shortly after and wondered what was wrong. When I told him what had happened, he told me that I hadn't done anything wrong. That evening Mrs. Jones called. Tim answered the telephone. She asked him if I was going to be coming in to work the next day. He told her that he was under the understanding that she had told me not to come back. She hung up. After a restless night's sleep and after waking up the next morning, I felt that maybe I needed to go back to Kiddie Kollege and try to talk to Mrs. Jones one more time. When I arrived at the preschool, all of my belongings were in boxes that were placed on the front lawn. I decided to pack the boxes in my car and go home.

I tried to file for unemployment, but because Mrs. Jones said that I had left on my own and didn't give her any notice, unemployment was denied. Tim and I both thought that this would be a good time for me to sign up for child development classes at MJC. I registered for classes that day. I knew that God was going to turn this bad situation into good. I had to believe that!

Three weeks after my last day working at Kiddie Kollege, I was able to find a job at a Christian Preschool. I had been calling all of the preschools in the telephone book and this place was looking for help right away. I was interviewed for the pre-school teacher position the next day. During the interview they asked me all of the usual interview questions, places I had worked, what my goals were, what my family life was about and what college classes I had taken. I explained that I had not taken any college courses, but planned to. They decided that they wanted me to come in the next day so I could interact with the children and so that they could see how I was with them. When I returned in the afternoon, all of the children were surrounded around a long table working with balloons, liquid starch and newspaper. It was a messy project, but I dove right in and I fully enjoyed it. I was there for two hours when Kathy, the Director asked to see me. She said that she thought I worked well with the children and that she wanted to hire me, but for me to work there I would need to get enrolled in Child Development classes. When I told her that I had already signed up for classes at the Junior College and would be starting classes within the next week, she was glad and told me that I didn't need to worry, they would work my hours around my class schedule. That was an answer to our prayers!

I loved my job! I loved working with the children and loved being able to share Jesus with them. I took child development classes at MJC in the early morning, went to work and then went back to MJC for night classes. It made for long days, but it was so fulfilling. One particular little girl that gave me so much joy was Holly. She was an energetic four-year-old with short, brown and curly hair, fair skinned and beautiful bluish green eyes. One day while out on the playground, Holly was jumping on a small trampoline. When I looked at her, I noticed that she had her hand against her pocket. The pocket was on the heart area of her shirt. It looked as though she was ready to say the Pledge of Allegiance. Curious, I asked Holly why her hand was on her heart. "Ms. Patti", she said, "Jesus lives in my heart and I don't want Him to jump out or fall out. I am keeping Him safe." I smiled and told her that she needn't worry about Jesus falling out. He was in her heart to stay. Although she was satisfied with my answer, she still had her hand against that pocket. A few weeks later, while we were eating a hot lunch Holly asked me if Jesus liked peas. I told her that I didn't know. She looked up at me with those endearing eyes as she touched her heart and said, "Well, He's probably hungry." As she ate a spoonful of peas, she chewed as fast as she could and then spurted out, "Ms. Patti, Jesus does *not* like peas!" Holly reminded me that when it comes to Jesus, things are simple. She embodied simple faith. The kind of faith that we all need.

I was able to get my Preschool Certificate within two years of taking child development classes. My original goal had been to be a kindergarten teacher, but after interning in a kindergarten class for three months, I saw that my heart was to be a preschool teacher therefore other than taking a few other classes, I ended my time at MJC.

After eight years of being married, Tim and I decided that we wanted to start a family. During this time, Aunt Linda had called and asked me if I wanted to go through some old photo albums and boxes that she had gotten out of storage. I did, so Tim and I took one afternoon and looked through them all. Looking through the pictures reminded me of all of those camping trips we went on and family holiday parties, etc. One box though held many official looking papers. Curiously, I looked through them. There was one paper that was headed Social Services with my name on it. As I read it, my heart raced. My emotions went all over. "I'm *not* crazy, It *is* true, it *wasn't* a dream." I got up and showed Tim the paper. What the paper, dated January of 1976 said was that after Donny and I were taken in by Aunt Linda and Uncle Joe, we had a physical and during the physical, I had been diagnosed with having untreated gonorrhea. I knew that meant that I had had sexual contact with someone, and besides Tim, there wasn't anyone else that I had had sexual contact with. *Other than Bob!* In an odd way, I was so relieved. Finally, I had proof that I had been molested. As I cried, Tim held me. I told him that I didn't just need to show Aunt Linda this paper, I had to! A few days later, with the paper in hand, I tried to talk to Aunt Linda about it. She just blew it off. She avoided giving me any response. I was upset and hurt over that. I chose not to bring it up again, until another time.

After diligently trying to get pregnant for two and a half years and not being able to conceive, our doctor referred us to a Fertility Specialist. We worked tirelessly through the fertility process for about two more years. Finally, a dye test was scheduled for me. A dye was injected into my body and an x-ray was taken, which showed that my fallopian tubes were severely scarred from having had gonorrhea that went untreated. All of our efforts to have a baby failed and abuse was the reason. Really? My childhood had been stolen from me and now Bob was stealing my hopes of being a mother away. How dare he! I was angry. I was devastated. I was hurt. I was fired up with head on emotions! After a couple of days, again I went to see Aunt Linda. This time with the test results in my hand. I had tears in my eyes as I tried to talk to her. She could see that something was obviously wrong with me. I told her that she knew that we were trying to have a baby for years and when I found the paper from Social Services and tried to talk to her about it she brushed it off. But now, how could she explain what the recent test result showed? When I said this, she put her head in the palms of her hands and cried. She told me that what had happened to me was all her fault. Her fault? I told her that she didn't abuse me, *Bob* did. She then said, "Patti, honey, if I had not introduce your mom to him then he would not have done that." I told her that she did not orchestrate what he did, *he* did and furthermore, if she had not introduced my mom to Bob, then I wouldn't have my brother and I would go through it all over again, if it meant that I would have my brother. She cried and hugged me tight. I now knew the reason why she felt she couldn't talk to me about what Bob had done. It still hurt me from deep within. I wondered why God would allow Bob to hurt me again. After much talking and praying, Tim and I decided that we would look into possibly adopting.

Tim and I lived in the triplex for about two years when someone from our church called to see if we would be interested in renting a country house from her parents. I was interested right away because one of the families in the triplex had *punk rocker* teens that lived right next to us. They had to walk by our unit to get to their unit. Their unit held parties at all hours and this group was rather colorful. They had bright colored spiked hair, wore bolt-type bracelets and chokers and dark make-up all of the time and their music was really loud. We could smell marijuana at all hours. I couldn't wait to tell Tim what our friend, Claudia, had called us about. He came home for his lunch break and when I told him about it, he wasn't the least bit interested because he thought that the rent would be too high. We were currently paying $400.00 for our monthly rent. He was in a hurry to leave, but I still wanted to talk about it. He said we could talk about it more when he came home from work.

Later, after Tim came home I was eager to try and talk him into moving. He decided that we should call Claudia and talk to her more about it. Claudia said that our rent would be the same as what we were currently paying, Tim was now interested, but not convinced. He was concerned that I would not be comfortable with living out in the country without any close by neighbors. I explained that it would be easier and probably safer than living where we were living. We drove out there and looked it over. It was a very old corner house on acres of peach orchards. It had two bedrooms, one bathroom, a large living room, kitchen, dining area, laundry room and a huge downstairs fully carpeted basement. Windows were all around the house. It held such character with its built-in nooks and a built in the wall ironing board. I loved it. The one car garage was detached and to me, it looked like we would have our very own parking lot. It also happened to be about three minutes to our church, rather than the twenty plus minutes that we were used to. Tim was involved in the sound ministry therefore we were at church at least two times during each week. We let Claudia know that we were interested, but added that we needed to pray about it for a couple of days. She was okay with that as were her parents, Wayne and Florence, who owned the house.

As we prayed about it, I recalled some things that happened at the triplex. I had met Tim there, we started our married life there and two other memories stood out. One was something funny, but endearing that Tim did. One Sunday evening during church, we watched a short video about a man who was asking for advice on how to add spark to his marriage. He was encouraged to be his wife's *Knight in Shining Armor*. The next scene showed the man walking up to his front door in a suit of armor holding flowers in one hand and candy in his other hand. He rang the doorbell. The wife, all frazzled, opened the door and immediately began crying. The husband asked her what was wrong. In a frantic voice she said, "The kids are not listening, the washing machine broke and spilled water all over the floor, I just burned dinner and to top it all off, you come home drunk." Tim thought the skit was so funny. He thought about it over and over. That should have been a clue to me that something was up. About a week later, I heard Tim pull into the garage. He took longer coming in than he normally did. Finally, I opened the front door that was across from the garage door to ask him if he needed any help bringing something in. Tim's voice stopped me. He asked me to go back into the house and said that he would be in the house in a few minutes. A few minutes later, the doorbell rang. I thought it was odd that he would be ringing the doorbell, but went and opened the door. I was shocked at what I saw. Tim had dressed himself in tin foil and he was holding flowers and candy in one hand and was reading from the Bible (the book of Song of Solomon, which is a love story). He was being my *Knight in Shining Tin Foil*. We laughed and laughed about it. I asked him why it took so long for him to come into the house. He told me that he was trying to think of a way to get into the house without the neighbors seeing him.

He has always had a unique sense of humor. And he has always been very romantic, leaving flowers on my car and having me go on scavenger hunts around our house that would lead me to love note after love note and often ending the scavenger hunt with an old love song that would be on a 45 rpm record that he would find at a record shop.

Another memory was about a time had given me an old reel to reel audio tape. It had a label with the heading of *Birthday Party at Hospital.* I had it for quite a while before I found someone who had a way of transferring it from the reel to reel to a cassette tape. When we were finally able to do this, fear struck me! I could make out every voice that I heard. My mom's weak voice, Aunt Linda, Uncle Joe, Aunt Tina, Grandma. Then there was a loud monstrous roaring type voice. It was almost as though you could hear the demon that Ken was possessed with. When Tim heard it, his eyes opened big. In a trembling voice, I said, "That is Ken! We need to turn that off!" Fear gripped me. I was shaking. Tim turned it off and held me. We decided that we would burn it. The metal garbage cans were set in the ground where we lived. The garbage had been picked up the day prior therefore it was pretty empty. Tim threw the reel to reel tape and the cassette tape into the garbage, lit a match and threw it in too. When the flame hit the bottom of the garbage, a flash flew up and smoke filled the area. To me, it looked like a demon had been neutralized! Oddly enough, I was glad that happened, because I felt that it allowed Tim to see the evil of Ken firsthand.

Our decision to move from the triplex to the country house came at a very busy time of year for Tim, Christmas time. We loved living in the country! It was quiet and the fragrance of peaches in the air during the summer was mouthwatering. We could mow the lawn at any hour, without disturbing anyone. A common thing to find where we lived was the dropping off of animals and furniture, and people didn't have any problem at all with trespassing and filling multiple buckets with peaches. We often intervened, but with so many people doing it, it was nearly impossible to stop. We had several stray cats and dogs over the years that we were there. I didn't mind at all, I've always loved animals. One night, I thought that there were cats on the porch. I went out to greet them and made sure they had food, only to be hissed at by a family of opossums. I was more careful after that. One winter, I heard a scratching sound in our bedroom wall. When I would hear it, I woke Tim up so he could hear it, but for some reason the noise stopped and he could never hear it. I knew it was there! Finally, one evening Tim heard it. He said that maybe one of the branches from one of the trees that was near the house was hitting the window and making the sound. I decided to go and look at all of the trees that were near our windows. It was winter therefore there weren't any branches so it wasn't possible for any branch to rub against any of the windows. The scratching sound didn't happen too often, but often enough. I would hear it when it was really quiet and when I would be getting ready for work or ready for bed. It seemed to be coming from inside the wall. Our bedroom drawers were attached to the lower wall in our bedroom and the long closet was above the drawers. I wondered if something could be stuck in my closet wall.

On the Saturday before Christmas, my family always has our family Christmas party. On this particular Saturday before Christmas, Tim was at work and I was getting ready for the party. I was getting ready in the bathroom when I heard that scratching sound again. "What could that be?" I asked myself as I cautiously began looking around. And there it was! Behind the toilet, there was a hole in the wall that was covered by a piece of wood, with a small opening. When I bent down and got a little closer, a claw came out at me. I screamed! As quickly as I could, I gathered all of my things. Make up, blow dryer, curling iron, clothes, shoes, telephone and then I hurriedly went downstairs into the basement, closing every door to every room on my way. Out of breath, I called Tim who was at work. I told him that he needed to come home, because there truly was something in the wall and its claw came out at me when I investigated the noise. He reminded me that he was working and that he would be home in a few hours and would check it out. "A few hours?" I thought. He told me to go out into the garage and get the bug spray and spray the hole behind the toilet. "What? Go back into the bathroom?" He told me that I needed to do it and that I could do it. After getting the bug spray, I sprayed the hole until my fingers ached. After Tim arrived at home, he decided to set off one of the smoke bombs that we had in the garage (we often had gopher problems). He put it into the ground and used a blower to make the smoke go further down into the gopher tunnels. There had been so many gopher holes, it looked like our entire yard had been smoldering from a fire that had just been put out. The animal that was in the wall of my bathroom, scratching on our bedroom wall was a gopher, and it was gone!

There was a six-week period that Aunt Linda stayed with us because she and Uncle Joe were still having their problems. She had closed her Quick and Clean business a couple of years after Tim and I were married and she was now working for a Credit Union. Out of the settlement that Uncle Joe received due to his back injury, together they bought real estate property in Riverdale, California. She had given the renters notice that they would need to move out so she could live there. Aunt Linda and Uncle Joe filed for divorce, he kept the house that they had shared together and she kept the rental house. It was hard on Tim, Aunt Linda and myself when Aunt Linda stayed with us. She liked to drink, smoke and make long distance phone calls. We didn't smoke or drink and we kept long distance phone calls to a bare minimum. We asked that she not smoke in the house. She said she wouldn't, but she did. Her dogs took over the house and our cat stayed clear of them. I loved those dogs so it didn't bother me too much. I wanted to honor Tim and I was also trying to find a way to honor my *mom, Aunt Linda*. It was hard. There were never any arguments, it was just hard trying to be a peacemaker to the two people that I loved the most. Tim understood and made a point of trying the best he could to be resilient and keep things light hearted. Aunt Linda made the move to her rental when it was vacated.

A couple of years after Aunt Linda moved to Riverdale, she became involved with Barry. She had known Barry many years prior to him going to prison. She started a relationship with him while he was in prison. She knew his whole family from when we were living in Hayward. I remembered his family, but I never recalled meeting him. Barry was younger than Aunt Linda. I didn't know much about him, other than he said that he had served time in jail. Aunt Linda thought Barry was rather handsome. He had a medium build and brownish/grey hair. He was about 5'8. He was a sweet talker. He could get along with anyone. He was also a partier. He didn't have a house or a job, other than doing small odd jobs for the job corps. Aunt Linda didn't have any problems with him living with her. They seemed to get along well enough. He came to family parties and interacted with everyone, but I was never comfortable with him. At times, he seemed to be a bit too friendly with the women he was around. I knew that I didn't ever want to be alone with him. After about a year, Aunt Linda and Barry were married. They were married in a small wedding chapel.

Uncle Joe stayed single after he and Aunt Linda divorced. Tim and I would visit him after church on Sunday's. At first, it was odd when we would see him because he would stay quiet. He wouldn't talk to me at all, only Tim. This bothered me. After leaving his house one Sunday, I asked Tim if he noticed how distant Uncle Joe was with me, he said that he did. I asked him what we should do about it. He said that we should pray about it. After talking to Aunt Linda on the telephone one day, I realized that she was hinting on if I was talking to Uncle Joe about her. I assured her that I wasn't. I also told her that I wasn't going to talk about him to her. She was understanding about it. While visiting

Uncle Joe the following Sunday, I was again given the silent treatment. My heart broke. Tim got up the nerve and told Uncle Joe that the reason why we went to visit him every Sunday was not because we were doing detective work for Aunt Linda, but because, "Patti wants a relationship with you. You raised her, you are her father figure and Linda is her mother figure. She knows she can't have a relationship with you both together. What she wants is a relationship with each of you separately." I told Uncle Joe that I loved him and that he would always be my dad and I would always respect his privacy. On this day, layers of distance fell from his heart. I gave him a big hug and he hugged me back. We began building a new and stronger relationship. His health continued to deteriorate. He now struggled with Type 2 Diabetes and had lost his leg from the knee down. He was heavy and pretty much bedridden. He drank a lot and alcohol was not his friend, neither were cigarettes and he was now addicted to his pain pills. His steady companion was his dog, Misty. She was a very smart Queensland heeler. Uncle Joe trained Misty to open his pill bottles and she was also trained to pick up his medication with just her teeth and carefully set the medicine tablets gently in his shaky hands. I was frustrated that Uncle Joe didn't take care of his diabetes. He was so good at encouraging me to take care of my diabetes, but he didn't have the motivation to take care of his. Truthfully, it made me angry, however I couldn't let him know. I just tried to love him and encourage him.

In the time that I worked at the Christian Preschool we went through three different Director's. I was hired by Kathy, who after one year quit to move on to another job field. Patty, who attended the church that the preschool was affiliated with became the Director. A few days after Patty arrived, one by one the preschool teachers left. No one had any reason to leave, other than we would be under new leadership and that meant that changes would be coming. I knew that I couldn't do that. I also knew that not all change is bad. I worried about how the preschool children and their families were going to feel if everyone that they were familiar with left. I also thought about how Patty was going to be able to get to know the children and their families without a familiar face that could make them feel more comfortable. I decided that I needed to stay. An additional teacher, Pat was hired a few days later. We now had two Miss Patti's and a Miss Pat. The children called me the *Old* Miss Patti because I had been there longer and Director Patty was the *New* Miss Patty because she had recently started. Both the parents and the children were confused because the *Old* Miss Patti was younger than the *New* Miss Patty. In time, more staff was gained, as well as new preschool children. Patty retired from being the Director after 17 years due to health issues she had. Miss Teri, who had been one of the pre-school teachers and later, the assistant director was now the Director. Teri's husband Bill was also a preschool teacher. All of the children loved Mr. Bill. He was goofy, funny and always happy. He was a great preschool teacher. He had a side job of being a party clown and he did awesome illusion tricks and made animals with balloons. He was a big kid at heart, which was an added bonus when it came to him being a preschool teacher.

Chapter 9

CONSIDERING ADOPTION AND REUNIFICATION

B ecause both Tim and I were shy, we thought that if we were going to have a family, we should probably move out of the farm area and into the city, where our kids would be able to have more friends and be able to interact more. We had been working with Family Connections Adoption Agency, but due to the cost of private adoption and after talking to some close friends at church who had adopted kids from the foster adoption program of Stanislaus County, we thought we would give that some thought. In the summer of 1996 we bought our first home. It was in a new development in Ceres. Tim's parents helped us with the down payment. We enjoyed watching our neighborhood being built. We had a small 1120 square foot house that sat on a corner. It had three bedrooms and 2 bathrooms, a two-car garage and a really nice front and back yard. The front yard was landscaped, but the backyard was not. I loved our little house. By the time we spent our first night there we were completely moved in and the house was all put together. Our finances were a bit tight because of our new endeavor, but God was faithful! One late afternoon, after Tim got home from work he mentioned that there was a lot of sod in the gutters of the houses that had been built around us. He thought that it looked like the sod had been discarded. He decided to ask the people who were landscaping all of the houses about it. They said that the sod in the curbside wasn't needed. Tim asked if he could take it off of their hands. They said it would help them if we did because then they wouldn't have to haul it off. What a blessing! Piece by piece, like a puzzle we managed to put our entire backyard together. We planted a fruit cocktail tree (that grew nectarines, plums and apricots), an orange tree, a plum tree and grape vines. When the trees grew and thrived they came in handy in the summer when we made refreshing smoothies! I also liked filling up bags with fruit and hanging them over our fence for our neighbors to enjoy.

In July of 1998, after coming home from work and bringing in the mail, I saw that I had a wedding invitation from New York. I opened it and saw that it was from my brother, Tom, who I had never met face to face. He and his girlfriend, Jessica were planning to get married that coming October. I showed Tim and said, "Wouldn't it be so funny if we went and sat in the back of the church? I wonder if anyone would know who I was." Tim said, "Let's pray about it." I thought, *"Sure, I'm really going to go there?"* Well, we prayed about it and went on about our business. Tim decided to call the airlines to see how much two tickets to Elmira, New York would cost. Including a hotel, the cost was $1,500.00 and that was something that we didn't have. Every Saturday Tim and I visited his mom and dad. They knew that we had been praying about possibly going to New York, however we never mentioned that it was our finances that held us back. This visit was normal but before we left, Ann handed us an envelope and asked us not to open it right then. She said that she felt like it was something that we needed. It was $1000.00. The following Monday, while I was at work, Patty called me into the office. I was a bit perplexed as to why she needed to see me, and a bit nervous. She congratulated me on being employed at the pre-school for 10 years and said that although it wasn't much, she had a check for me. After thanking her, I looked at the check. Not much? She had no idea what this exact amount of money meant to Tim and I. It was $500.00. God had indeed supplied the $1,500.00 that would be needed to buy two airline tickets to Elmira, New York. Tim was so thrilled! He told me that it looked like God wanted us to go to New York. Guarded, I asked him, "What if no one but my brother wants me to go to New York?" We decided that I would make some calls. I first called Aunt Linda, then Uncle Joe. I asked them what they thought about me possibly going to New York. I had not shared with them anything about the invitation beforehand. Aunt Linda was pretty surprised about it. After giving it some thought, she said that if we were soon going to be taking foster care-adoption classes and getting ready to hopefully adopt a child then she thought that it would be a good idea for us to go to New York. "Now, God," I thought, "this is too easy." I called Uncle Joe and he too thought it would be a good idea for us to go. I also called Aunt Tina. She liked the idea, but understood my hesitation because years ago when I had called my dad, he told me not to call him again. I wondered out loud if he would even want to see me. I called my brother, Tom. When I told him that we were thinking about coming to his wedding, he was pleasantly surprised. I then explained to him that this day was his and Jessica's day and I didn't want to take any attention from them. He said that if he didn't want me to be there, then he would not have sent the invitation. I told him about my worries about our dad. He encouraged me to call him. Because

I still wasn't comfortable with doing that, I called my grandma, Grandma Casey instead. When I told her who I was, she screamed so loud into the phone that I had to move it away from my ear.

"Really???? Patti, you are going to come to New York? Really??? Does Jimmy know about this?" I let her know that I had talked to Tom, but not my dad. She urged me to call him right then! "Right now?", I thought to myself after hanging up the phone. I mustered up all of the courage that was within me and very slowly picked up the phone and with shaky hands, I pushed in his phone number, ever so slowly. It rang once, twice, three times. Maybe he wouldn't even be there.

I was just about to hang up when I heard a distant, "Hello??" It was *him*! "Hello?" he said again. I said, "Hello, this is Patti." "This is Patti?" he said. He was surprised to hear my voice. We made small talk. He asked how I was, what my interests were and if I was happy. I answered his questions. I then told him about the wedding invitation I had received from Tom. He seemed surprised and asked if I was thinking about going to the wedding. I told him that I hadn't decided for sure yet. He wanted to know why I hadn't made a decision yet. I told him that we didn't know if we could afford it, but after praying about it, God provided all of the money for the trip. I told him that I had talked to my family to see how they felt about it and they all encouraged me to go. I let him know that I had also talked to both Tom and Grandma Casey and they both encouraged me to go. I then told him that I wasn't sure how he would feel about it.

"How would I feel about it?" he asked, "I would love to see you."

"You would?," I asked.

He said, "Why do you ask?" I explained to him that years ago, when I was 14, I called him on Father's day to wish him a Happy Father's Day and he told me not to call him anymore therefore I didn't. He went silent. He finally said, "I am so sorry, 'I don't remember that, I was drinking bad back then, please think about coming, I would really like to see you." I told him that I would talk to Tim about it.

Tim was Praising God big time! He said that he had been praying about this for so long and it seemed that when he redirected his prayers, asking God to reunite families back together, "God did *this!*" He was so excited about what God was doing. I was now beginning to get somewhat excited. How did I allow myself to ever doubt that God would do this? That is the God we serve. He longs for restoration and reunification and for families to be put together however I have to say that I still let my insecurities get to me.

Soon after, we began trying making flight arrangements and hotel reservations. Both

Grandma Casey and my dad had offered for us to stay with them but I didn't feel comfortable with doing that. I thought it was important for Tim and I to have privacy and that it would allow me the ability to deal with whatever emotions that might come up. I also wanted to be able to freely talk about how I felt.

The day had finally come. We were packed and ready to begin a new journey in our lives. I was so nervous. Tim nor I had ever flown before and our first flight was to meet my New York family. When we arrived at the San Francisco Airport, we were relieved because we had just tackled very heavy traffic at the Bay Bridge. Thankfully, we arrived one hour before flight time, as was required. It took two planes to get to Elmira and there was a flight delay in Philadelphia. On the flight, I don't know what I was more nervous about, the flight or meeting my dad. The second plane was much smaller than the first. This made me even more nervous. The flight attendant could tell I was nervous so she engaged me in small talk. She asked us what the purpose of our flight was. I shared that I was going to meet my dad for the first time since I was 2 years old and watch the brother I've never met get married. She thought that it sounded exciting. I told her it was scary. She wished us luck.

We arrived in Elmira, New York at 11 pm. As we walked out of the plane and through the corridor,

I held tightly onto Tim's hand. I was tired, scared, nervous, excited and terrified. And then there they were. Grandma Casey, my dad, my brother and my soon to be sister in law, Jessica. Grandma Casey called me by my mom's name, "Judy, look at you." Then she corrected herself and told me that I looked so much like my mom. I didn't realize how much I looked like my mom until they told me over and over again. I gave Grandma Casey a big hug and she held me tightly in her arms. She told me to go and say hi to my dad. I went to him and gave him a guarded hug. He hugged me back and kissed my cheek and said that it was good to see me. I then hugged Tom and Jessica. Those hugs were much easier to give. It was decided that we would all meet at my dad's house after Tim and I rented a car at the airport. We arrived at my dad's house at 12:30 am. It was awkward to say the least. We were all tired and really didn't know how to open up a conversation. We were offered something to eat, but declined. My dad had his hands in his pants pockets as he paced up and down his hallway with his head down. My heart was racing. I asked God for His peace and at once my heart opened up.

My dad nervously looked at me and said. "You probably have a lot of questions for me."

I told him that I didn't. I said, "Well, I thought I did but after giving it more thought, I feel that it is important to know that when there is a divorce and kids are involved, there are not two sides to a story, but three, and sometimes more if there are more kids." I then nervously said, "If you don't mind, instead of looking back, I would rather look ahead and begin building a future with you starting today, *if* that's okay with you."

He looked at me in surprise. "*If* it's okay with me? "It sounds like a perfect plan to me." At that very moment, I saw his entire demeanor change. His shoulders didn't appear to be so heavy, his brow wasn't sweaty and he seemed to have more confidence. He was right, I did have many questions that I wanted to ask him but I didn't want to hinder what I felt God was doing and I didn't feel the need to dredge up the past.

This wasn't at all easy for me to do. You see, I had to let go of my need to gain validation and for him to feel bad for what had or not happened between us. Doing that would not allow us to grow a new relationship. And again, I sure didn't want to hinder what I knew that God was doing. He enabled me to want to move forward and not backwards and I wanted to do my best to follow His lead.

The next day, we visited with the whole Casey family, including Aunt Kathy, who was my dad's sister and her husband, Uncle Lee and their daughter Kasey. While at Grandma Casey's, she told me about her late husband, Grandfather

Casey. He was a well-known chef. She also talked about how she had always hoped to meet me. She showed me the baby pictures that she had of me that were nearby in old picture frames. My dad took out his wallet and pulled out an old and tattered newspaper clipping of me being announced as possibly being the 200 billionth American born and a picture of me with him standing outside in a parking lot. He told me that he always kept those keepsakes close to him. This brought tears to my eyes but I wiped them away in order to keep myself composed. He also shared with me how very much he had loved my mom and I. He drove us to the house that my mom and Uncle Mike had lived at with their dad. He told me that my mom had a violent dad and my mom's dad had hurt her many times. He said that he thought my mom fled from her dad to be with him to be safe. I was learning new things about my mom. We had lunch together and my dad told us that there was no need for us to have a rental car. He said that he would take us wherever we needed to go, therefore we took the rental car back to the airport rental place.

Tom and Jessica's wedding day was the next day. The wedding was beautiful. I felt honored to be there although I was uncomfortable when it was announced that *Tom's sister from California* was there. It was then announced that Tom wanted to share a dance with me. I have always strongly disliked being the center of attention so I know that during the dance I must have turned at least ten different shades of red. It was a moment in time that I will cherish for a lifetime.

Our visit in Elmira, New York lasted three days. After our visit, something happened. Layers of hurt began to peel off from me. I felt like an onion with layers of skin being pulled away and like a new me was being formed. A new me filled with confidence, hope and even boldness. Tim has shared with me that he thinks that because I was given the feeling of being fully accepted by my dad and we were able to start a new relationship, it caused me to change. He said that was when I was able to come out of my shy shell. I couldn't have praised God more for His perfect plan in piecing together my relationship with my dad. I looked forward to the next phase of our relationship.

Chapter 10

A RESTORED RELATIONSHIP

My dad and I kept in close contact and talked on the telephone at least twice a month. He was interested in every detail of my life. He would ask me about my work, church and anything that Tim and I may have been doing since the last time that we had talked. He was retired and shared about the things that he did with Grandma Casey. They spent a lot of time together and he drove her wherever she needed to to go. Grandma Casey called me about twice a week. She shared the similar stories that my dad had shared with me and she would talk about her church. She loved getting together with "those saints", she would call them.

One day in the mail, I received a small package from Grandma Casey. I was puzzled when I opened it. It was a little metal loop that had a soft bristled cushion around on one end. Grandma Casey wrote on an index card, "Something you probably have never used but might really need to use." There were two, one for Tim and one for me. We were stumped. We thought maybe the item was to clean our ears. I decided to call Grandma Casey and ask her what the gft was that she sent. She asked me if I read the cards. I told her that I had only received one card and I read her what was on it. "Oh", she said, "I must have forgotten to put the other card in there." After a long pause, I asked her, "Well Grandma Casey, can you please tell me what the other card said?" "Oh, the other card? Oh yes, the card said, *"Belly Button Cleaner.*" She went on to say that the Saints in her Sunday School class made them for their families and we needed to use them. Tim and I both thought that it was odd however we did as she asked and used them, but only one time.

On holidays and my birthdays, my dad called me at 12 am his time, 9 pm my time because he wanted to be the first one to wish me a Happy Birthday, a Merry Christmas, etc. We were getting closer. Tim and I decided to make plans for a future visit to Elmira.

After taking some time and realizing that not only were there kids in other countries who needed to be adopted, there were also kids in our own backyard who were needing families. We called the County Foster Care Program and a short time later, we began Foster Adoption classes. We went through background checks, home inspections, and listened to countless speakers talk about their experiences with adoption. Some stories were scary, others were encouraging and still others were heart wrenching. We filled out page after page of information about ourselves and pictures of us were taken so they could match us up with children. That was when the waiting began.

After meeting my dad and building a relationship with him, we planned to see him again a year later. We had our airline tickets paid and were anticipating our trip when the County called us about placing two boys with us, with the intention of adopting them. We went the next day to meet 5-year-old Joshua and 3-year-old Brandon. They were adorable. They were biological brothers and they had two sisters and one brother who were in foster care homes. When trying to adopt through the County, their first priority is to reunite families back together. After making sure that the parents have taken classes on parenting and after taking the steps to ensure their child's safety and well-being, the children are reunited with their families. We knew that, but we also knew that some families were not able to reunite and at that time the children would be available to adopt. We knew that we wanted the boys but we had already planned and paid for our trip to Elmira. We prayed that God would make it possible for us to be able to change our flight and change our vacation days, making it possible for us to still be able to get the boys. Tim called and pleaded with the airlines. He told him our dilemma and the strict timeline that we were on. We needed a miracle! After much pleading and praying, the airlines moved our flight. Praise God! We now had to focus on finishing up the room that Joshua and Brandon would be sharing, we needed to find them a bed. The night before we were to leave for Elmira, Tim and I were at a shopping center and as we walked by a furniture rental place, we saw bunk beds through the store window. We decided to go in and take a look at them. We were surprised to see that they weren't for rent but for sale and the mattresses were included. They were in good shape and the price was good therefore we bought them. We went home and set the bunk beds up. Now the boys' room was ready for them and we were ready for our trip to New York.

The airline flight was not as nerve wracking this time. Again, we were asked by a stewardess the reason for our flight. She enjoyed our story about how we needed to change our flight plans because when we returned home, we were going to be blessed with two boys.

Our trip to Elmira was nice. My dad took us sightseeing and to meet some of his friends. We also spent a lot of time with Aunt Kathy, Uncle Lee, Kasey, Tom, Jessica and Grandma Casey. Tim and I were able to enjoy a few nice walks. The air there was clean and the colors of nature were vibrant and rich in color, it was almost breathtaking. The second morning that we were there my dad made breakfast for us. We had pancakes, sausage, bacon and eggs and toast with juice. I'm not a big eater but I did eat one small pancake, one sausage link and a piece of toast. I didn't take much insulin because I didn't eat very many carbohydrates. About 15 minutes after breakfast, Tim and I decided to go for a walk. It was a nice morning for a walk. There weren't any fences around any of the houses and there was a quiet calmness. We wore light sweaters due to the air being a bit cool. As we walked, we thanked God for how He orchestrated every detail of me reuniting with my dad. We knew that we could not have planned it any better than Him. We also prayed for God's wisdom and guidance as we were about to be parents to Joshua and Brandon. As we approached the bottom of the small road that we were on my legs began to lock up. Each step I made jerked. I fumbled as I tried to stay upright. Tim caught me and asked me if I was okay. I told him that I thought I was but I didn't know what was happening with my legs. Suddenly, I fell to the ground. Tim realized that my blood glucose dropped and we were in an emergency. A woman driving by asked us if we were okay and Tim told her that I was a diabetic and that I was having an insulin reaction and he needed to know where the nearest store was so he could get me some juice. Thankfully, the store was just a block away. The kind woman stayed with me as Tim ran to the store, bought a container of juice and hurried it back to me as quickly as he could. After drinking it, within a couple of minutes I was better and my legs stopped locking up. For some reason, while we were in New York, I didn't need the doses of insulin that I was used to, I needed less so I lessened my insulin doses and made sure that I had a box of juice with me at all times. We made our way back to my dad's house, spent time talking about our new adventure of taking Joshua and Brandon in, relaxed, played cards and later we all went out to dinner with the rest of the Casey family. We packed that evening for our trip home the next day.

A few days after we were home from Elmira, we picked up Joshua and Brandon from the County office. I was both nervous and excited. They were excited too. They had been with an emergency family until a foster-adopt family was found. They loved their room that they shared and screamed with excitement when they eyed the toys in the corner. Joshua had an athletic build and had beautiful brown eyes, brownish blonde hair, and a smile that could light up a room and charm the socks off of you. Brandon had an adorable little pudgy body with brown hair, brown eyes and he had a contagious giggle. Joshua and Brandon were active boys. They loved rough playing, playing with any type of ball and they loved to run around anywhere they were. Because I was a preschool teacher they were able to go to the preschool with me. I wish that I would have been given some time off to bond with them. They called us mommy and daddy right away. We found out that Joshua and Brandon had been neglected. We were told that their mom and dad had done drugs. The older girls tried to feed the boys and care for them but they were little themselves and needed someone to take care of them. CPS was eventually called and all of the children were taken away. Their mom spent months in a Women's Home. About once a week a County Counselor would come to our house and talk privately with both Joshua and Brandon. We had to document any injuries or outbursts that the boys may have had. After about two months, we had to take the boys to the county office to meet with their mom for an hour twice a week. This was hard for me. I felt like maybe I was going to lose them. They called both her and I mommy, including our first names. She made it to just about every meeting.

Tim taught Joshua and Brandon how to ride bikes, they loved it. Because they were so energetic, we went to the park often to fly kites, play catch and run, run, run and we went to Tim's parents house to swim often throughout the summer.

Because we felt that it was important for Joshua and Brandon to be able to have some sort of contact with their sisters, Felicia and Christina, we contacted their foster parents and scheduled lunch dates at parks and fast food restaurants at least once every other month. They all loved getting together.

About eight months after we brought Joshua and Brandon home with us, their mom was able to have them for the weekends. She was still living at the Woman's House therefore the weekend visits were there. At first the boys were excited about it, but after they realized that they wouldn't be able to go to church with us because we couldn't pick them up until Sunday afternoons, they were sad. This broke my heart. The boys counselor still came to meet with them once a week, bringing toys and stickers with her. After 16 months, their mom successfully earned her parental rights back and regained custody of Joshua and Brandon. Great accomplishment for her, but a huge heartache for me. I remember packing their things together and trying to hide my sadness from them. Joshua brushed up against me and asked me what was going to happen if they were hungry and didn't have food or if they were hurt and couldn't feel better. I held him and told him not to worry and that I would always be praying for him and Brandon and would always be there for them. I then took a permanent marker and wrote our telephone number in the tongues of all of his shoes. I told him that if he needed us, I would search high and low for him to bring him back to safety. That seemed to ease his mind. I had the day off from work and on Tim's lunch hour we met together at where we were going to drop off the boys. Joshua and Brandon hugged us and I couldn't help but let my tears fall. Tim went off to work and I drove myself home to a very empty house, but not before pulling over a few times because my tears were making my vision blurry. In the quiet of my home, I asked God why I could not have any children. I asked Him why I had to hurt so much. I was absolutely crushed. I prayed for Joshua and Brandon daily and I also prayed for their mom. I prayed that she would be able to be the mom that these boys needed and deserved.

We were advised not to have any contact with the boys after they were reunited with their mom. It was thought that it would confuse them. I didn't like that, but I understood. We were also told that if their mom couldn't take care of the boys, we would be called and they would come back to us and we could move on with adoption. I didn't want them to go back and forth. I trusted that the right decision had been made and tried to be at peace with that.

The County Foster Care Program called us a few times about us taking in other children. We received a call about a 3-year-old little boy, a sibling group of three and two young boys—one was 3 years old and the other was a 5-month-old baby. We met them, however I wasn't interested. I had a hard time opening my heart again, only to be disappointed. I know it wasn't fair to the children for me to feel this way, and for that reason I just couldn't say yes. Tim was disappointed that I didn't want to move forward with trying to adopt again. At one time he made the comment, "Who are you waiting to adopt? Jesus? He's already taken." I told him that I didn't know. It just hurt so much to lose Joshua and Brandon. I needed God to heal my heart. I needed God to bring me guidance and direction. I prayed for this every day. I often wondered if they were okay, if they were being cared for, if they were happy, if they missed me. I knew that I missed them terribly.

My dad decided that he wanted to come to California with Grandma Casey. He had known my grandpa, and all of my aunts and uncles and now he was comfortable with getting together with them. My dad and Grandma Casey made the trip to California in the summer of 2000. They stayed with Tim and I for four days. We enjoyed a big family picnic at a park. Everyone enjoyed each other's company. Grandma Casey was really smitten by Grandpa Tomasetti and she wasn't shy about him knowing it. Whenever she was near him she would say, "You know what the Bible says, "Greet one another with a holy kiss" (2 Corinthians 13:12 NIV) and that's exactly what I am going to do." At that moment she gave him a great big kiss right on his lower cheek, causing Grandpa to blush. He seemed to enjoy the attention. On another day, my dad asked if we could go to the Chapel of the Chimes Cemetery, where my mom and grandma are buried. Aunt Tina, Uncle Rick, Uncle Mike and Grandpa went with us. My dad was very emotional when we were there. While he wept, he tried to hold his composure, but it was hard. I went to him and we held each other for a short while. He brought two roses. He placed one on my mom's burial site and one on my grandma's burial site. A short time later we went to look at where my mom and Uncle Mike had once lived. My dad recognized it right away. I could see that many memories were coming back to him. On the way back to my house, he was pretty quiet. I respected his privacy.

When Grandma Casey realized that a nearby town had an A&W restaurant, she was adamant that we go there and have a root beer float. She was amazed when she saw that the meals were still delivered as she remembered, by girls on roller skates right up to the car. Such joy was on her face while we were there. When she saw that there were root beer float lollipops she was so excited and bought a bouquet of them to take back to Elmira with her.

The last day we were together, we all stayed home and relaxed. We played cards, looked through picture albums and talked about our hopes for the future. My dad told me that he was very proud of me and was so glad to have me back in his life. With tears, my dad said that building a relationship with me was a great gift to him. That meant a lot to me.

On the way to the airport the next day we wondered who would visit next, him or us. We also wondered how long it would be before we would see each other again? We hoped that it would be soon.

Tim and I still talked about the possibility of being parents someday but deep down inside my heart, it seemed like hope was fading away. As much as I loved Aunt Linda, she had a way of not thinking before she spoke. In other words, she often had a foot shaped mouth. During a time when there were two people in our family that were expecting babies, as well as a couple of friends, she called me one day and asked me, "How does it feel that so many people around you are pregnant and you can't get pregnant?" Tears streamed down my face as I was reminded of what I couldn't do–get pregnant. Other times, it would be little things that were said, "I wonder what you would have done, if you had a baby and it did that (whatever she was seeing a child doing)," or, if a conversation on kids came up, I may have had some input due to being a preschool teacher, but she would let me know that speaking as a teacher was different than speaking as a parent. Comments like that pierced my heart. I learned to be quiet and expect those jabs. Tim talked to Aunt Linda about it a few times and it would get better, but not for long. I know she didn't intentionally mean to hurt me with her words, but she did.

Uncle Joe's health continued to deteriorate due to his chain smoking, alcoholism and not taking care of his Type 2 Diabetes. After he had a leg amputated because of complications with his diabetes, he became very sad. It was hard for him to get used to wearing a prosthetic leg. He said it hurt and it was uncomfortable and hard to walk in. He wasn't good at following doctor's orders and keeping up with his physical therapy. He continued to drink and smoke and overtake his medication. He put on a lot of weight, making it very difficult for him to get around. I believe he just wanted to give up. The chronic back pain that Uncle Joe suffered caused him to rarely sleep at night. His company was the shopping channel on tv. He was always finding *good deals, buy one get one free, or buy one get two free deals*. He would barter with people and trade things with them. There were a few occasions when we were visiting him that he would say that he thought he had something that we needed. We always told him that we already had everything we needed. He would smirk at us. One time he asked, "Do you have a coffee pot?"

"No", I told him.

"Then you need one," he told me, "Go to the back bedroom and go to the far slider closet, open the door and the second stack, third box down is the coffee pot that I want you to take home with you." Again, I told him that we didn't need one because we weren't coffee drinkers. "Well", he said, "One day you might be or maybe you will have some company that will want to enjoy a good cup of coffee. Now, go get that coffee pot." I obeyed and sure enough the box that held that particular coffee pot he was talking about was right where he had said it would be. We took the coffee pot home with us and every time we have a family get together, I get out the coffee pot and smile, remembering his precise detail and him making sure that I had what he thought I needed.

Uncle Joe would at times ask me about Aunt Linda. I think that he knew that her marriage wasn't very happy by talking to Auntie Verla. Auntie Verla was still very close with both Uncle Joe and Aunt Linda. Barry was very controlling and would try to manipulate his way through whatever he could. It seemed that he played on Aunt Linda's sympathy daily. He was dishonest, he was an alcoholic and he seemed to lack motivation to work but did not have any trouble at all with people offering their help to him. People thought they were helping him, but I think what they were doing was enabling him to manipulate more people. When Tim and I were around him he would seem nice enough, but I felt that something was definitely off with him. I decided not to allow myself to be alone in a room with him. Unbenounced to anyone around me, I set up safety boundaries around myself.

Aunt Linda often asked about Uncle Joe. She knew about his health problems. They talked a few times on the telephone and she went to see him one time while he was in the hospital. They both enjoyed their time talking. Neither of them realized that they were gifting each other with something that one of them would soon come to treasure.

Chapter 11

THE MOST PRICELESS GIFT

O n my birthday, November 20, 2002, it was a pretty uneventful day for the most part. My birthdays were just like any other day to me. Tim and I were ready to turn in for the night when the telephone rang at 9:30 pm We rarely had calls at 9:30 pm or later, other than my dad and he already had called at 12 am (New York time and 9:00 pm California time). I listened as Tim answered the phone. His words were, "Yes, really, okay, when and I will talk to Patti and get back to you." It could have been someone from church or one of our friends or a family member but not any of those crossed my mind. As Tim listened intently to what the person on the other end of the telephone was saying, his face showed many emotions. I thought by now that the person he was talking to was our Social Worker, Karen and I thought that she was probably talking to him about kids who needed a home.

At one point I looked at him and said, "Okay, let's do it."

"Do what?," he asked.

"Go to the County office and meet the kids," I said. He was pleasantly surprised at my response. He let Karen know that we would be there by 1:00 the next day. When he hung up he asked me how I knew who was on the phone and what the conversation was about. I told him that I just did.

The next day we met Nate-Paul who was almost 4 years old and Allison who was almost 3 years old. My heart melted when I looked at them. Nate-Paul had long brownish/red hair with bangs with brownish/green eyes. Allison had brownish blonde hair. It was choppy all over like it had been cut in chunks. Her eyes were baby blue and her left eye had a little bitty freckle in the color of her eye, setting her apart from anyone else. My heart sank when I came up close to her. Her body was greyish in color. I was told later that it was due to the bad bruising that she had suffered, which was the reason they had been put into the Foster Care system. Allison and Nate-Paul were removed from their home October 25, 2002. The bruises were fading. She also had some fading bruises on her stomach. Despite all of this, I felt such warmth in my heart when I met them. Karen was with us, along with Larry, who was a CPS worker. He was the one who had been called to investigate and possibly remove the children from their birth mom. Nate-Paul was on the floor playing with cars and Allison was sitting near a chair with a book on her lap. I squatted down and sat in a chair at their level and tried to strike up some small talk. At first, they were both shy but after a few minutes they warmed up and talked with both Tim and I, they even sat in our laps. At one point, Allison picked up the chair that she had been sitting near and lifted it over her head and began walking in circles. Nate-Paul called out to her, "Sissy, put that down." She smiled at him but went about her merry way carrying the chair above her head a little longer. Nate-Paul took out more cars and made all of the vroom vroom sounds and honking and crashing sounds that he could.

We stayed for about 30 minutes then made our way back to Karen's office. She told us that their father was on the run and if he returned he would be locked up for running from an honor farm. They were fairly certain that the mother was the one responsible for Allison's injuries. They said that they would need to provide her with services to help her get off of drugs and provide parenting classes for her to go through. Again, I had to understand that us having the children may only be temporary. Karen went on to say that because they were doubtful that they would be able to achieve a successful outcome with the children's mom, they made the decision to place the children in a foster adoptive home. We were told that Nate-Paul and Allison's great grandparents were too old and their paternal aunt was too young to care for them and their grandma was ruled out due to her criminal history. This was a lot for us to take in. As Karen walked us out, she and Tim were walking side by side down the corridor and I was walking a step or two behind them. Karen told Tim that she knew it sounded rushed, but she would need to know by noon the next day if we wanted to move forward with Nate-Paul and Allison. I called out, "Okay, I'm ready." They didn't appear to have heard me.

Tim looked at me and in a louder voice said, "Karen needs to know our answer by tomorrow."

I said, "Okay, I am ready, yes!" Tim was shocked. He reminded me that I had turned down three other opportunities that we were called about. When he asked me if I was serious, I smiled at him and assured him that I was. We told Karen that minute that we were ready to move forward. She was surprised at such a quick response. We talked to Karen the following day about picking the kids up from the respite home in order to spend some time with them prior to them coming to live with us. She mentioned that Larry had some reservations about how Allison and I had interacted with one another. Larry was very protective over Allison. Karen said that she assured him that the visit we had with Nate-Paul and Allison went very well and that she was very comfortable with placing the children with us. Although Larry was reluctant, he agreed to move forward, trusting that Karen was right. I have to say that I was very hurt about the reservations that Larry had. I wondered and wondered what I could have done to make him feel the way he did. Karen assured me that she didn't see anything wrong with the visit and she thought that Larry was being overprotective since he was the one who had removed them from their home.

After talking things over with Karen, we called Catalina, who was the foster mother that Nate-Paul and Allison were with. She had provided emergency respite care to them when they were removed from their home. We asked her if we could pick them up one day that week and take them to get something to eat and go to the park. She chose a Wednesday night. When we picked them up it was pretty cold out. We went to McDonalds for dinner and then we went park hopping. We stopped at every park we could think of and we played and played and had a great time. Both Nate-Paul and Allison were very energetic and they were also very competitive. We ran, went on slides, went on the swings and chased each other. After about three hours, we took them back to Catalina's house. They were tired out! We asked Catalina if it would be okay if they spent the following weekend with us. She was okay with it. On the way home, Tim and I talked about what we would soon be doing. We were cautiously excited. I told Tim that we needed to do some shopping, because we didn't have any girl toys for Allison to play with and that we needed to get some boy toys too because what we had wasn't much. We agreed that we would go shopping the next night. I had a hard time sleeping that night. I wondered if it was because of all the excitement that I was feeling?

One thing that was constantly on our minds was our finances. The County reimbursed us for all of the clothes that we had bought the kids the day we went shopping in anticipation of having them for the weekend, which was a nice blessing. They also let us know that they had the kids on Medi-Cal, another blessing. We knew that raising kids was expensive. After praying about it and talking to each other about our new life with kids, we were reminded that if everyone who wanted to have kids waited to have kids until they could afford them then no one would ever have them. We knew that we had to keep trusting God with this. The next day, I went to work and asked for enrollment papers for Nate-Paul and Allison. Thankfully, because I was employed by the preschool, we were blessed to be paying half price for the kids to be in preschool- another blessing. Everyone was so excited for us, but they also knew that the possibility of what had happened with Joshua and Brandon could possibly happen again. This was hard to recall. I decided not to think about that happening again. I couldn't!

The day came for us to pick up Nate-Paul and Allison. It was a Friday afternoon. When we arrived to pick them up they ran into our arms. They were so excited. We had pizza for dinner and we watched Veggie Tales videos. Later, they had fun taking a bubble bath together and they couldn't wait to put on the new pajamas that we had bought for them. When we tucked them in that night, Nate-Paul and Allison were somewhat nervous therefore after we said good night prayers, we put a night light in their room. They slept soundly.

Tim and I stayed up talking for a little while before we went to bed. We talked about *our kids*. *Our kids!* As we lay in our bed we could hear them sleeping. Slow deep breaths and a few sighs. We couldn't help but to go look in on them. They were peacefully sound asleep.

We were awakened the next morning with little footsteps trotting down the hall. It was time for breakfast! They were too little for our big dining room table therefore we piled telephone books on the chairs so they could reach their bowls of cereal. The telephone books began to slide and Nate-Paul and Allison decided that that wasn't comfortable. Later that morning we went shopping for a kids table, just their size. We also went to Tim's parents house and introduced them to the kids. They were a bit shy at first and stuck close to us, but they warmed up in no time and chatted away.

On the way home that day, I asked Nate-Paul if his real name was Nate-Paul or if it was Nathan or Nathaniel. Allison joined in the conversation by saying, "He Nate-Paul." Nate-Paul paused a bit then said that he liked the name "Nufaniel" (Nathaniel) and decided that was the name that he wanted to be called. From then on, we called him Nathaniel. When we arrived home, I looked at Nathaniel and Allison and told them that I loved them.

Nathaniel asked, "How much?" I was caught off guard by the question.

"How much?," I asked. "Up to heaven and back," I replied with a smile.

"Wow," Nathaniel said, "That's a whole lot." I agreed. That phrase began to be the staple phrase of our love for each other. Also on that day, Nathaniel and Allison began to call Tim and I, "Mommy and Daddy."

Sunday morning was completely different than what we had been accustomed to since losing Joshua and Brandon. We explained to Nathaniel and Allison that we were going to go to church.

They asked us what church was. We explained that it was a fun place to go where they could play, sing and learn about God. That was good enough for them. I was a little nervous about going to church with them, because I knew that my church family had witnessed my sadness with losing the boys. I wondered if they thought that I was going to lose Nathaniel and Allison as well. Nathaniel and Allison both wanted me to carry them in and that made me so happy. Yes, little me carried both of them. They loved Sunday School. On our way home, they asked if we would be going there again. They cheered when we told them, "Absolutely!"

On Sunday evening, we took the kids back to Catalina's house. They were sad about it and so were we. When we spoke with Karen the next day, it was decided that Nathaniel and Allison would come and live with us the following Friday-December 6, 2002. They were so excited when we picked them up. They were glad to be sharing a bedroom. Nathaniel had superhero bedding and Allison had Hello Kitty bedding that my friend Heidi gifted them with. They jumped on their beds, hugging their very own pillows. They settled into our home and into our hearts with such ease.

On Monday, Nathaniel and Allison began pre-school where I taught at the Christian Preschool. They fit right in. Because I had the 6:30 am opening position, they had to be up pretty early each morning. My day ended at 1pm, Nathaniel and Allison were exhausted on the way home. When we walked in the door, they flopped onto their beds and took a good two-hour nap. They would have slept longer, if I let them. I woke them up at 3:30, gave them a snack and then they had the choice of playing or watching cartoons. By 7:30 pm they were ready for bed. Tim and I both tucked them in at first. But the tuck in time would have the kids wrestling with Tim therefore I decided that Tim could do the tuck in time on his own. I would say my good night's to them before they went into their room.

Because we were told by Karen that we would be taking the kids to visit their mom twice a week beginning this first week that we had them, my emotions were up and down. The visits were during Tim's lunch hour therefore he picked them up from preschool and took them. I met them all at home afterwards. The meetings were an hour long and they were in a small room at the Social Services building. Their mom didn't come to many visits, but their Nana, who was their paternal grandma and their paternal Aunt Emily came. There were a couple of times that their maternal grandma came. Tim and I decided that we should buy a video camera so we could take video of the children while they were still little, because we knew that time would pass by quickly. After getting the video camera, Tim requested permission to videotape one of the family visits that their biological mother came to. He thought that it would be important to have this video so that as Nathaniel and Allison grew up, they could watch it and see their biological mom and family. I was reluctant, but understood the reasoning behind it. There were a few occasions that I took them to the visits. I sat in a waiting room while they visited. A child counselor came to our home at least once every two weeks to talk with the kids. It was at this time that I would be asked about injuries that may have happened or about any kind of emotional outbursts that may have occurred. Everything had to be documented.

After about a week of Nathaniel and Allison being in our home, we needed to take them to get a physical. While we were in the waiting room of the Medical Center, we filled out medical papers as the kids played. Tim and I were doing our best to answer the questions that were asked on the paperwork that we were given. As we did this, one of the doctors walked by. When he saw us, he came to an abrupt stop and a look of amazement was on his face. He later told us that he was the doctor who had examined the kids when they were removed from their home. He said that Allison had been in pretty bad shape. He was so pleased to see her looking so good.

The next thing we had to do was get them looked at by a dentist. Allison had three cavities and Nathaniel had a total of nine cavities. He was going to have to have quite a bit of work done in his mouth. Poor little guy, I could relate. An appointment was made for their dental work to be done. The appointments were about 35 minutes away from where we lived. Because Nathaniel and Allison were so little and wiggly, they had to be sedated. Tim took them and while he was there he called me and told me that Nathaniel would need to have caps on his two front teeth. He explained that the porcelain ones were very expensive, but the silver ones would be covered by the insurance. Silver caps is what we went with. When they came home Nathaniel smiled and showed off his *silver stars*. He loved them! He asked for some yogurt, because he was hungry! It was hard to eat though, because his mouth was still numb. Nathaniel came to really like those caps. When his front teeth later became loose, he was devastated, because that meant that he was going to lose his stars.

I loved being a mom! I loved that both Nathaniel and Allison loved cuddling. There were often times that the three of us would squish ourselves together on the small loveseat in our living room and watch tv. They enjoyed having their backs rubbed, so they would lay on the couch with their heads on my lap and watch tv, while I caressed their backs.

One evening, Allison became very interested in the earrings that I had been wearing. She played with them gently then noticed the hole that was in my ear that was holding my earring. She decided that she wanted to have holes in her ears like mine. She asked us when she could get it done. Tim and I told her that she could have her ears pierced when she was four years old. That pleased her. We thought that she would forget all about it, but she didn't. Two days before her fourth birthday, Allison declared that it was almost time to get her ears pierced, because she "would be four years old in two more days." We made good on that promise.

We were initiated into parenthood pretty quickly. About three weeks after they were with us, while we were at church, Nathaniel and Allison were in the 3 & 4-year- old Sunday School class. Tim and I were enjoying the worship service when an usher came up to us and tapped Tim on the shoulder and said that one of our kids needed us. As we casually stood up, we were told that we needed to hurry, because Nathaniel was bleeding pretty badly. I had Tim walk ahead of me to see what was wrong, because the sight of blood caused me to be queasy. By this time, Nathaniel was in the nursery with someone holding a towel over his thumb. His thumb was bleeding badly. When we walked into the room Nathaniel called out to me, "Mommy." Tim lifted him into his arms, while asking what had happened. We were told that he had been running around in the classroom and as he was running, his thumb became caught in a rivet of a metal folding chair and he yanked it out and vigorously shook it, splitting his thumb open and causing his blood to splatter. We rushed him to the Emergency room, where he had to have stitches put in. He screamed so loudly, it tore my heart out. He had to wear a bandage around his thumb for about a month.

About three weeks after the bandage and stitches were out of Nathaniel's thumb, as he was playing in the play yard at preschool, he was walking and one of his feet tripped over the other foot and he tumbled down, hitting the left side of his forehead on the rounded curb that separated the cement from the bark area. It was a hard hit, he was screaming as I quickly ran to him. When he looked up at me, I could see a lump forming and his forehead change in color to a deep dark bluish/purple. I took him inside the preschool and put a cup over the lump and used medical wrap to keep it in place. I first went to Tim's work, because he had the Medi-Cal cards. When Tim came out I tried to tell him what happened, but something else caught his attention. Gas was leaking out of our gas tank. Because my focus was still on Nathaniel, I continued to persist to try and tell Tim what had happened and that I needed to get

Nathaniel to the doctor ASAP. He explained that if we didn't fix what was wrong with the gas tank we may not make it to the doctor, due to the van exploding. That scared me enough to catch my attention! It was decided that we needed to take the van back to the mechanic who had worked on it a few days prior. When they found that there was a loose gas line, they repaired it quickly. Nathaniel was not crying during this interruption, but I could tell he was hurting. Tim gave me the Medi-Cal card and when I told him what had happened, he went to Nathaniel. When he removed the cup from Nathaniel's forehead, he was shocked at what the wound looked like and firmly asked me, "Why didn't you tell me it was *this* bad?" I told him that I tried. Tim saw that the lump on his forehead was about the size of a tennis ball and because he needed to get back to work, I took the kids to the Emergency Room. There wasn't a long wait. Nathaniel was given an MRI on his head. He didn't want to be in the MRI machine. He cried, but he was more peaceful when they told him that I could be nearby and that he would be able to hear my voice. We prayed together. Praise God that the MRI didn't reveal any abnormalities. He just had a really big lump on his head that would prove to be a real attention getter!

That Christmas, our first Christmas was so much fun! I don't know who was more excited to get up on Christmas morning, Nathaniel and Allison or Tim and I. We got up first. I wanted to make sure all of the Christmas lights were on and that the Christmas praise music was playing before the kids came through the living room. The look of surprise on their faces when they saw all of the gifts under the Christmas tree was priceless! We explained to them that before we opened gifts we wanted to read to them the story of Jesus' birth from the Bible. They were a bit disappointed, but listened. The big hit of their Christmas was getting their own bicycles with training wheels. Nathaniel also enjoyed a remote control car and Allison a baby doll with a baby stroller, along with many other toys that they received.

The kids really enjoyed our family Christmas parties. My family and Tim's family always celebrated Christmas on different days, which always made it convenient for us. The Saturday before Christmas, my big family would gather together and exchange gifts. On Christmas Eve, Tim and I exchanged gifts with Aunt Linda and Uncle Joe, but since their divorce we would go see Uncle Joe in the early part of Christmas Day and the rest of Christmas Day was shared with Tim's family.

The monthly visits still went on. After a few months, it was evident that the biological mom was not going to be able to regain custody of Nathaniel and Allison and the visits at Social Services with the family would soon be ending. The ones who just about made it to every visit they could was their Aunt Emily and Nana Clara. During one visit, while we were all together visiting and playing with the kids in the playroom at Social Services, Emily, with tears in her eyes told us that she could see that the kids were well cared for and that they were happy. She told us that she thought it was best for them to stay with us. Nana Clara agreed. Emily then said that if they could, they would still like to see the kids, if it was okay with us. Tim and I had already talked about it. We had decided that it would be best for Nathaniel and Allison if they did see Aunt Emily and Nana Clara, because one, they were responsible in keeping up with the County visits and two, because they would still have some biological family familiarity. It was decided that we would meet at McDonald's every three months or so.

After having Nathaniel and Allison for 13 months, we were called into a meeting with Karen and she congratulated us and told us that we were now free to adopt Nathaniel and Allison. All four of us were absolutely elated! We cheered and hugged each other. A date was set to legalize the adoption—March 30, 2004.

A week before the adoption, some final paper-work needed to be filled out. Social Worker, Roger went through all of the papers with us. He showed us the new birth certificates that Tim and I would be named as Nathaniel and Allison's birth parents. I wept. "Was this real?," I wondered to myself. Tim took my hand and squeezed it three times (from early on in our relationship, three light hand squeezes has meant, *"I love you."*) Roger could see my array of emotion.

Roger said, "Long time coming, huh?" I nodded my head yes. He knew the road we had been traveling was a hard one over the past couple of years. As he finished up the last page of the paperwork he asked us if we wanted to be a part of the AAP Program. We had never heard of that program and we asked what it was. "You never heard of that term?," Roger asked us in a surprised tone. We told him we hadn't. He explained that it was the Adoption Assistance Program and, if we wanted it, we could still continue to be paid as we were when we were fostering the children and they could still receive Medi-Cal for their medical and dental needs.

"Yes!", we told Richard, we would love to be a part of the AAP program- another blessing. He had us sign the papers and then he was gone.

On March 30th, 2004 at 11 am, we became the proud parents of Nathaniel and Allison Robinson.

My long-awaited dream came true. In attendance were Aunt Linda, Grandma Ann, one of our Pastors, Pastor Dave (who my kids had named Papa) and his wife, Pam (who was called Mema), Karen and Roger. My heart was full!

My dad had been excited about our news of us adopting Nathaniel and Allison. Sadly, he was never going to meet them, because after 4 years of us reconnecting, he passed away. As much as my heart broke at the loss of my dad, I was thankful that a few months before he passed away, he told me how he had come to admire my faith and my willingness to forgive him and he asked me if I would help him ask God to be in his life. With grateful tears in my eyes, I led him in a sinner's prayer and listened to my dad as he asked Jesus into his heart.

The prayer that I had my dad repeat after me went something like this- Dear God, I admit that I am a sinner and I need Your forgiveness. I believe that Jesus Christ died in my place paying the penalty for my sins. I am willing right now to turn from my sins and accept You, Jesus as my personal Lord and Savior. I commit myself to You and ask that You send the Holy Spirit into my life, to fill me and take control, and help me to be the person you want me to be. Thank You Jesus for hearing my prayers and loving me. In Jesus' Name I Pray, Amen."

It broke Grandma Casey's heart when she lost my dad. They were so close. She and I talked on the telephone at least three times a week. She wanted to come back to California to see me. She talked Aunt Kathy and Uncle Lee and Kasey into accompanying her. They came that June and they stayed with us. They loved Nathaniel and Allison. Kasey was seven years old. She was an only child, she seemed to enjoy playing with her new cousins. Grandma Casey seemed to have an agenda. She wanted to meet Tim's parents and she wanted to hopefully see Uncle Mike and absolutely see Grandpa Tomasetti again. We also went to the park and flew kites.

On our way to Dublin, California to see Grandpa, we were driving on the freeway when Grandma Casey observed cows lying down in the fields. She declared, "Rain is coming!" It was a nice sunny day, so I asked her why she would think that rain was going to come. She said that "When the cows are lying down, that means rain is coming." Low and behold, a little while later on that sunny day, it rained. I have seen cows lying in the field since then and rain didn't always come. I think God allowed Grandma Casey to be right in that instance. She was pretty impressed with that. We enjoyed visiting with Grandpa and again, she greeted him with a *holy kiss*, and he welcomed it with a smile. Uncle Mike and Aunt Claudia were divorced now and he was hard to find because since the divorce, as much as our family tried to help him, he had chosen a life of homelessness. Thankfully, he was around when Grandma Casey visited and she was able to see him and love on him. She shared with me on this trip that her life was complete because I was in it. She and I grew very close.

The visit with my New York family came to an end four days after they came. Before they made their way to the airplane, Grandma Casey embraced me in a long tearful hug. I had no idea that that day would be the last hug that I would ever receive from her. Grandma Casey lived to be 89 years old.

Chapter 12

CANCER STRIKES AGAIN

While Grandma Casey had been visiting, we noticed that Aunt Linda didn't look very well. She said that she thought she was coming down with something. I called her the day after my family left. She sounded weak. She said that she was going to see her doctor in two days. The next weekend she broke the news to me that she had lung cancer, I was devastated. I was angry. She said that she was going to start chemotherapy soon. I told her that I would accompany her and she was adamant that I didn't. She said she did not want me to be with her during that time, because it would be too painful for her to see me endure the emotion that it would take. I didn't like it, but I respected her wishes, but only when I found out that someone else would be accompanying her. It was her cousin, Rhoda. The chemo was harsh on her. She and Barry were not together anymore, but he was still around. He made her feel like she needed him.

We spent a lot of time with Aunt Linda. We brought her dinners and she enjoyed being with Nathaniel and Allison. When Aunt Linda's hair began to fall out, she cried. She then took out an electric shaver and shaved her head. The next day, Lisa was in town (she was living in the mountains about three hours away and Tony had moved with his family to Idaho) and she took Aunt Linda wig shopping. Aunt Linda bought a short auburn colored wig. She was self-conscious as she wore it, but she learned to be comfortable in it.

In late August, I began asking Aunt Linda what kinds of things she had always hoped to do but had never had the opportunity to do. After much thought, she said that she had always wanted to go on a cruise. That gave me an idea. I called Aunt Tina and told her what Aunt Linda had said. We decided that because Aunt Linda's birthday was in October, we would throw her a big birthday party at Aunt Tina's house. It would have a Cruise Theme. Everyone who was able donated money and two cruise tickets were bought for Aunt Linda. She could take anyone she wanted, but we already knew it would be Barry. Tim and I created a huge treasure chest and asked everyone to write cards and/or letters to her about how they felt about her or how she had impacted their lives. Aunt Tina bought Aunt Linda's favorite candy bars and had a ship logo wrapper put on them with her birthdate and name. Her favorite candy was Hershey bars with almonds. She had taught me when I was little to find the perfect Hershey bar with almonds by gently rubbing the back of the candy bar and finding the one with the most almonds. For every holiday since that time, I always included a Hershey candy bar with the most almonds with every gift that I gave to her. This night though, she would receive the extra-large Hershey bar with almonds with the gift I gave to her. We invited everyone in our family and extended family. We had a barbecue and an array of food all around the house. We made sure we had Coca Cola, her favorite soda. Many people attended. By evening time, Aunt Linda looked very tired. She and I took some time and went to a quiet room to just be. I told her how very much I loved her and I thanked her for taking Donny and I in so many years ago. It was such an unselfish thing for her to do. I knew that it was hard on her. She smiled at me and told me with tears in her eyes how proud she was of me and that if we had to go back and relive that time, she would do it all over again. She also told me how thankful she was that I had Tim as my husband. She said that if she could have hand-picked a man for me, it would definitely be Tim.

As the evening moved on ahead, Aunt Tina set a majesty type chair in the corner of the living room for Aunt Linda to sit in and everyone gathered in a circular formation around her. Everyone took turns reading their card or letter to her out loud. She was taken aback by all of the memories that people had of her extending herself, her home, and her care to them. She laughed and cried at all of those memories. Then my letter came. It was about six pages long. My letters and cards were always long and everyone knew that therefore they had me read mine last. She was overwhelmed with emotion that night. After we finished reading our cards and letters, we set them inside her treasure box, not realizing the impact that those treasures would have on her and even me at a later time. We then presented her with her gifts. First, she was presented with two tickets for a Catalina Island four-day cruise. She was shocked. All of the other gifts that she was given were items that she could take on her cruise or things that she could enjoy at home, like flavored coffee, nail polish, candy, crossword puzzles, word searches, country music cd's, books, lap blankets and an electric neck massager. Aunt Linda was set! It was indeed a night to remember! Lisa and Tony made it to the party. Aunt Linda had no idea that they would be there. Donny was in the Air Force and was not able to come. Barry was distant that night.

Because Aunt Linda's cancer continued to spread quickly, she was unable to go on the Catalina Island cruise. She was getting weaker and weaker. We talked every day. Sometimes it wasn't for long, because she was so weak. Other times it was longer. One afternoon when I called her to ask how her doctor appointment that she had earlier in the day had gone, she was crying and told me that she couldn't talk to me and then she hung up the telephone. "She can't do that to me", I thought and I called her back. I asked her what was going on. She said, "Honey, I'm okay, I'm just sitting here looking up at all of my cards and letters from my birthday and I can't believe that so many nice things were said about me." Rhoda had put up a fishing line from near the ceiling of her living room from one corner of the wall to the other corner of the wall and she hung all of the cards and letters that Aunt Linda had been given over the fishing line. She spent a lot of time looking at them and recalling all of those good times.

Barry seemed to have been taking care of her. When we were at her house for Thanksgiving, everything seemed okay. He was getting her things when she asked for them and he looked like he was making her as comfortable as she could be. Yet, at times when I would call and check on her, she often said that she didn't know where Barry was. By early December, Hospice was involved in caring for Aunt Linda. They tried to have her live out the rest of her life the best that she could. They helped her to not be in pain and made sure that she was cared for appropriately.

The weekend before Christmas while I was visiting Aunt Linda and was sitting at her bedside, she asked me to close her bedroom door because she had something that she needed me to know. After I closed her bedroom door, she pointed at her tall jewelry box and told me that she wanted me to have it and that I could do whatever I wanted with the jewelry. Most of it was costume jewelry. She then pointed to the top right-hand closet area and said that there were 5 fanny bags and five little purses, one for each of her ten grandkids and she wanted to make sure that I gave the grandkids those items. She explained that they would all have $100.00 waiting for them in their fanny bag or purse. She had them hiding under a stack of pillows. She also told me that she put a stash of money under a floorboard in the bathroom. She told me that when it was time, I needed to take it and use it for whatever I needed to use it for. I listened to her, but didn't respond much. I didn't want to think about losing her.

Aunt Tina and Uncle Ron thought it was time to call Donny home on emergency leave from the Air

Force because it was apparent that this was going to be our last Christmas with Aunt Linda. Aunt Tina and Uncle Ron graciously paid for Donny and his family to come home. Lisa didn't live too far away therefore soon Aunt Linda would have Lisa, Donny and I with her. All we needed now was Tony.

The Wednesday evening before Christmas Aunt Linda was in good spirits and she was sitting upright on the couch in her living room. She was weak, but able to communicate and even make a few jokes. Uncle Ron had a computer program with a will kit on it. Aunt Tina had talked to Aunt Linda about it and they decided together that tonight Aunt Linda would have Uncle Ron document her wishes. The people in attendance were Aunt Linda, Barry, Aunt Tina, Uncle Ron, Lisa, Donny and his wife Kathy and Tim and I. At first it was uncomfortable small talk. Aunt Linda told us all that after she passed away, Rhoda was going to do her makeup. She explained that she had shown Rhoda how to do it. This was important to her, because she had the bad memory of how my mom had looked at her funeral. She mentioned that she had looked like a clown and didn't want that to be the last thought people had of her. She then asked me if I would paint her nails. With tears, I told her that I didn't think that I could do that. I told her that I would be grieving too much. I knew that I couldn't do that! The conversation moved onto finances and how she wanted things to be distributed. Barry was quiet and at times, he drifted to sleep. She mentioned that she wanted Barry taken care of and her dogs taken care of. We knew that Barry had not been around much and he had not treated Aunt Linda right. We asked her if she was sure about what she wanted to leave Barry. She responded that she knew that he didn't deserve anything but that she wanted to at least know that she did everything that she could do to make sure he was taken care of. That was the kind of person Aunt Linda was. She never stopped caring for people and she always looked out for others, no matter what the people around her thought about it. We all asked her again if she was sure about what she wanted to do for Barry and she said she was sure. Uncle Ron now had it all documented. She named Tim and I as the Executors of her will. The night was draining. Afterwards, we all enjoyed banana cream pie, Aunt Linda's favorite.

On Thursday we had a Traveling Notary come to Aunt Linda's house. Aunt Linda was even weaker than she had been the day before, she had a hard time signing her name on her legal papers but she was well aware of what she was doing. Tim also called a local funeral home and made an appointment for us to make preliminary funeral plans.

On Christmas Eve Day, Aunt Tina, Donny, Tim and I talked to the Funeral planners at the funeral home. It was so hard and emotional. We chose a coffin, the burial site, stationary, etc. Donny made the down payment. It was a hard task, especially since 29 years ago that very day my mom was buried. Our emotions were pretty raw.

Christmas Eve night, just as we have always done we went to Aunt Linda's house and exchanged gifts. She loved the soft, rose colored robe that we bought her so much that she put it on. She smiled when she eyed the Hershey bar with almonds in the gift bag and as she caressed the back of the Hershey bar, she looked at me and I saw a tear flow down her cheek. I scooted closer to her and caressed her hand. She made small talk with Nathaniel and Allison. Aunt Linda was more alert this night than any of the previous days and she was in good spirits. It was almost as if she was getting better. She had a houseful of loved ones—Donny, his wife Kathy, Aunt Tina, Lisa, Barry, Rhoda and Tim and I and our kids. When we left that night, we were thankful that she was doing so well, but we were all a bit concerned because Lisa planned on staying the night with Aunt Linda and Barry. Lisa and Barry did not get along at all, but they decided to try to make peace for Aunt Linda's sake.

On Christmas morning, Nathaniel and Allison were up early. We read the beloved Christmas story out of the book of Luke (2:1-20 NIV) from the Bible and the kids opened up their Christmas gifts. We were busily getting ready for the day. Our plan was to go to Tim's parents for a short while, then go and spend some time with Aunt Linda. We were making a big pot of chili when the telephone rang. It was Lisa and then Barry. They were arguing. Lisa said that Barry came on to her and touched her inappropriately. Barry wanted us to help get Lisa out of the house. Aunt Tina called us asking us what was going on, because either Lisa or Barry had called her and left a message. We were trying to piece it all together. Aunt Tina called Uncle Bill, who lived nearby and asked him to go to Aunt Linda's to see what was going on. We dropped our kids off with Tim's parents and rushed over to Aunt Linda's. When we arrived, two Hospice nurses were waiting outside, along with a Sheriff's Deputy. Uncle Bill had told Lisa to leave and go to his house and wait there. Uncle Bill extending the invitation to Lisa to go to his house did help to bring a sense of peace, although Barry was still upset and pacing outdoors. This gave the Hospice nurses the opportunity to go in and provide the proper care that Aunt Linda needed. Because of the heated arguing between Lisa and Barry, the nurses had decided not to go into the house. We swiftly made our way into the house and I went straight into Aunt Linda's room. I was absolutely shocked at what I saw. Aunt Linda's lifeless body was lying there on her bed and she was whimpering. Her lips were badly cracked and she looked so thirsty. Her eyes were dark. She had a sponge straw sitting in a small cup of water by her bedside. I wondered why Barry hadn't been quenching her lips. As I lifted the sponge to her mouth, she sighed. I was so angry! As upsetting as this was, I realized that this outrageous situation motivated most of our family to get to Aunt Linda's house as quickly as possible.

After the Hospice Nurses evaluated Aunt Linda, they reached the conclusion that she was nearing the end of her life and would most likely pass away around 5 pm that day. There was a vigil around her bedside throughout the day, with people praying, crying and singing songs of worship. At this point Aunt Linda could no longer talk, all she could do is gently squeeze our hands to indicate yes or no. In the meantime, Tony and his family had begun driving from Idaho that morning in hopes of getting to Aunt Linda before she passed away. Later in the day, Lisa came back to the house to pick up her belongings, said her goodbyes to Aunt Linda and headed back home to her home in the nearby mountains. As it was getting closer to 5 pm, Tony still had a ways to go before getting to Aunt Linda's house. Fortunately, 5 pm came and went and Aunt Linda was still with us. At one point, I recalled how Aunt Linda had gone to church with us and she had really liked the song, "Open the Eyes of My Heart Lord". Those of us around her bedside began to softly sing it to her. Her breath was getting faint, but she was holding on. We thought she was holding on for Tony. She had seen Lisa, Donny and I, but not Tony. I prayed that he would make it. At 6:30 pm, Tony and his family made it to Aunt Linda's. Tony rushed into Aunt Linda's room and ran to her bedside and held her in his arms. Most of the room cleared, I stayed near. After a few minutes Tony and I held each other. We hugged for a long while. We then sat at Aunt Linda's bedside and talked quietly to her. At about 6:55 pm, after she acknowledged Tony, Aunt Linda took her last breath and a piece of my heart broke apart as she was peacefully escorted to heaven by God's angels. To me, it was like time stood still.

We stayed in Aunt Linda's bedroom until it was time for the Hospice nurse, who had been at the house all day to come in and pronounce her deceased. A blanket was put over her body. I still held her hand. I cried as I held her hand. I was so angry at Barry for not taking care of her on the last day of her life. I was also angry at cancer. How dare it take another person from me.

There were still many people at the house. Barry wanted to go into the bedroom that Aunt Linda was in. When he did, I left the room. I didn't want to talk to anyone, I just wanted to grieve. I went to a corner in the living room, near the back sliding glass door and sat on the floor behind the end table. I stayed away from everyone and just cried. After about twenty minutes or so, my eyes spotted photo albums in the bottom of the end table that I was sitting by. I pulled them out and looked through each one. Not like I normally did, I spent a lot of time looking into each photo, remembering all of the details of each photograph. As I did this, I felt the need to start collecting every picture that I could and box them up to take home with me. I also took the graduation pictures of Lisa, Tony, Donny and I off of the wall and took them. I had an overwhelming feeling that I *had* to do this. Tim at one point stopped me and asked me what I was doing and why was I doing it. I explained that I felt an urgency to take pictures home. He told me that he thought that I shouldn't do that, "After all, it is still Barry's house", he told me.

"No", I said, "It is Aunt Linda's house." Tim said that Barry still lived there though. I understood Tim's line of thinking, but I still asked him to just trust me. I think that the other people in the house also thought that I was being insensitive. I just couldn't shake this feeling. Barry never asked me what I was doing.

At about 9:30, the Coroner came to pick up Aunt Linda's body. We watched them take her body out of the house on a gurney, and then she was gone. Our family mourned together for a short time and then we each went on our way to our own homes. Tim and I picked up Nathaniel and Allison, who were sound asleep. I was glad that they were able to spend Christmas Day at Grandma Ann and Grandpa Richard's house. It would be so hard the next day to tell them that Grandma Linda had passed away and was now in heaven. When we did, they had a couple of questions. Did she hurt? Would they see her again? They were really sad.

The next day, after church we went back to Aunt Linda's house. We had a key. We were shocked at what we saw. The house had been cleaned out. Barry had given everything away to people we didn't know and I was pretty sure that Aunt Linda didn't know either. All of her knick knacks were gone. I went into her bedroom to get those fanny bags and purses for her grandkids and the money in the floorboard of the bathroom that she had told me about and it was all gone, even her jewelry box and all of her clothes. "What was Barry doing?" I thought. The house looked desolate. Barry was not at the house. Rhoda came by while we were there. She was also shocked at how the house looked. We talked to Rhoda for a while and then she handed me Aunt Linda's purse and a ring that Aunt Linda had a jewelry store make for her twenty plus years prior. It was a diamond and ruby ring.

Aunt Linda loved the ring so much. I was glad to have it.

Auntie Verla kept in close contact with us over the telephone. She now had a caregiver living with her named Danny. When I called Aunt Verla and told her about Aunt Linda, she didn't say a word, she just wept. When I called Uncle Joe, he did the same. We talked to Lisa and Tony and because Tony was in town, we were going to try to get the memorial service planned right away. Lisa told us that she preferred that the memorial service not be on New Year's Eve, because she had plans. I told her that we would do our best.

On Monday afternoon, Tim and I went to the funeral home and made plans for Aunt Linda's memorial service. While we were there we also had the obituary for the newspaper filled out. This process was much easier than it should have been, because we had just been there three days prior to making these preparations, just in case something happened. We didn't realize that she would be gone the next day. That was the timing of God! The scheduling of the memorial service was difficult. We were trying to plan it for the following Friday, but the schedule was already full. The only day open was New Year's Eve. So, that was when we had to have it. Now we had to tell Lisa. She wasn't happy about it. I felt really bad about it and told her that we did our best however there wasn't any availability for the few days before New Year's Eve day or the week after.

Uncle Ron and Donny used most of the pictures that I had brought home from Aunt Linda's house the night she had passed away to make a dvd tribute of Aunt Linda's life. The music that was played on the dvd was "I Can Only Imagine" by Mercy Me and "If You Could See Me Now" by Know. They are both beautiful songs about being in the presence of God.

The memorial service was absolutely beautiful. Aunt Linda looked stunning. Rhoda did a fantastic job making sure Aunt Linda looked like herself. In fact, to me, it looked like Aunt Linda was just asleep, not gone. Lisa, still angry that Aunt Linda had included Barry in her will decided that she wasn't going to come to the memorial service. Tony wasn't happy about Barry being in Aunt Linda's will either, but he knew that was what his mom wanted. He and his family were able to attend the memorial service before they headed back home to Idaho. While I sat alone with my grieving tears at the memorial service before the service began, I realized something. Aunt Linda passed away knowing how people felt about her through the letters and cards that she came to treasure. How many people go through their lives not having any idea of the impact that they have made on someone's life or the difference they made? I made a promise to God that day. I promised that I would not let a day go by that I would not try to speak hope, truth and love into someone's life. I try to make good on that promise every day.

Soon after Aunt Linda's memorial service, Tim and I sought help from an attorney to begin the process of settling Aunt Linda's estate. Lisa and Tony still wanted to make sure that Barry didn't get anything from her estate. As much as I didn't want Barry to have anything either, we had to follow what her will stated. It was a very long and stressful process, but in the end we were able to fulfill most of what she wanted. We were learning as we went because we had never done anything like this before. During the process, Barry was still living in the house and it was Aunt Linda's desire to purchase a mobile home for Barry from her assets however he couldn't qualify for the rental agreement in a mobile home park. Because of this, he asked us if we would purchase a used motorhome for him. We had to get this request formalized by the attorney. Lisa and Tony contested this change to the will, which was going to save Aunt Linda's estate a large sum of money, but because they contested it, we had to spend additional money to get this change approved. We found a buyer for Aunt Linda's house and had a set date to hand the keys over to them. Barry assured us that he would move out when he needed to, but he wasn't putting much effort into looking for a motorhome to move into. We decided to serve Barry with an eviction notice. It was going to take time for the eviction process to play out, which would have put us well past the date that we were supposed to hand the keys to the house over to the new owner. At this point it had been seven months of stress, worry and frustration and the house was one of the last major hurdles that we needed to overcome, and now this was in jeopardy. We began crying out to God for His help with this, as we had done so all throughout this entire hardship. It was a huge toll on our family. When life gets turned upside down by major life events, life doesn't pause. It just continues on, which means the responsibilities of parenting and working were still a big part of our daily lives. As we continued to seek God for His wisdom, He led Tim to to Exodus 14:13-14 (NASB), which says, "but Moses said to the people, "Do not fear! Stand by and see the salvation of the Lord, which He will accomplish for you today; for the Egyptians you see today, you will never see again. The Lord will fight for you while you keep silent." Tim felt like God was speaking to him personally about Barry and the house. Within the next two days, Barry found a motorhome, which we purchased and then he was out of the house. This allowed us to hand over the house to the new owner on time. God is good!

At the conclusion of settling Aunt Linda's estate, all of her bills were paid and there was some money left to divide up between Lisa, Tony, Donny and I, as well as Barry. However, because Lisa was so upset that Barry had been included somewhat in the money that had been divided between all of us, she severed her relationship with me. I wish that I could have kept Barry from gaining anything, but that is not how Aunt Linda had instructed me to do things. As much as I didn't agree with what Aunt Linda wanted, I had to honor her wishes.

After about 10 years, Lisa and I reconnected through social media. We gained a distant closeness of sorts. I am sad to say that she passed away a few years later from having had colon cancer. She proved to be a true warrior by letting go of the past and living her life out the best that she could.

Once the estate was complete, I looked into grief counseling with Hospice. The grief counseling classes were held once a week. Tim and I signed up to go and Tim's parents agreed to babysit for us on those evenings. The first class we went to, I was surprised to see one of the Hospice nurses that had cared for Aunt Linda. I thought to myself how nice it was for her to be there to offer her support to me. After we each introduced ourselves to each other and why we were there, I realized that she was there because she had been grieving a sister that she had lost three years prior. When it was my turn to share, I was still pretty raw with emotion and I was still very angry with Barry. I shared all of my feelings. Something happened for me that night. The Hospice nurse who I thought was there to support me told me something that I didn't realize how much I needed to hear. She validated how I felt about how Barry had treated Aunt Linda those last couple of days of her life. She said that she had been a nurse for Hospice for years and she had never seen a scene like she had on that dreaded Christmas day. I needed to hear that so much, because I thought that maybe, just maybe, I had been too overly sensitive. I hugged her and thanked her for validating me.

Chapter 13

DARK MEMORIES EXPOSED TO THE LIGHT

I worked at the Christian Preschool for 17 years, until I was laid off. I had felt that God had been nudging me to move on from there for a few years, but I kept making excuses. The layoff came as a surprise to me. I was not the only one laid off. A fellow teacher, Vanessa was also laid off. We were both devastated. Thankfully, within about a week and a half God blessed me with another preschool job. I was now working at another wonderful Christ-centered Preschool. Vanessa was also hired right along with me there. I was glad to have the opening position, just like I had had at the first Christian Preschool. I have always enjoyed being able to greet the parents and preschool children at the start of the day and hopefully bring them a sense of joy as they begin each day. I taught the 4 and 5 year olds. The name I have always had

for my class is *The Sunflower Class,* because sun-
flowers always face the sun, it reminds me that I
also need to always face the Son of God.

Over time, sleeping at night was hard for me.
Night terrors were invading my sleep. Grueling
night terrors. I would wake up panting, like I had
either been running from someone or something
or fighting someone. Tim would try to wake me,
but had a hard time. It was even harder for him to
wake me up if I had had a night terror during a low
blood glucose insulin reaction. When I would wake
up, I couldn't recall anything that had happened.
Tim decided that at night he would play a tape of
praise songs with scriptures. I didn't know he did
this until months later. I couldn't get a scripture
out of my mind and I knew that I didn't know the
scripture by heart. When I shared this with Tim, he
smiled and showed me the cassette holder of the
music he had been playing for me each night. The
scripture had come from the music he had been
playing each night. My subconscious had been
soaking it all in. Tim also shared with me that my
night terrors didn't happen as often as they once
did. I continually wondered why I had those night
terrors and asked God to help me figure out why I
had them, but I did so with caution.

On my 40th birthday, while at work, Vanessa asked me what I was going to be doing for my birthday. I told her that I didn't have plans to do anything. She asked me again and I replied the same way. Then she raised her voice and asked, "Why is it that you not only don't want to celebrate your birthday, but you also don't want anyone else to celebrate you on your birthday either?" As I looked at her, trying to put together a response, a cascade of memories overcame me. I excused myself and went to the staff bathroom in shock at what I was remembering. I remembered my 8th birthday, being at the hospital with my mom. I recalled everyone who was there. I remembered a little white wind up ballerina music box. I also remembered the dreadful night that followed and all of what Ken had done to me—the bath, him hitting me with a branch from a tree, and those dreadful spiders. After I cried my eyes out and composed myself, I went back into work, as quiet as a mouse. On the way home from work, as I thought about everything, I became angry, mad and hurt. Now, I realized why I was so afraid of spiders and I realized why I never liked my birthday. I wondered why God allowed for all of what had happened to me to happen.

When Tim came home from work, I unloaded all of what happened on him. He held me and said that he was sorry. I told him that the Bible says in

Luke 17:2 (NKJV) "It would be better for him if a millstone were tied around his neck, and he be thrown into the sea, than he should offend one of these little ones", "and God let both Bob and Ken harm me, why?" Tim explained that we live in a fallen world and that evil happens and everyone has free will and sometimes people use that free will to do harm.

I stopped him from talking. "Free will?" I asked. "I wasn't given a choice. I didn't want that abuse to happen. I reasoned that God let them do what they "chose to do", so He must not love me enough to save me." Tim tried to reassure me, but I clammed up. I decided that I didn't matter to God and I was mad. I went into about a week-long depression. I didn't have any joy. I didn't let any light come into the house or into my life. I didn't listen to Christian radio and I kept all of the blinds tightly closed. I didn't read my Bible and I couldn't pray, not to a God that didn't think I mattered. About 5 days into that depressed state of mind, on a Sunday morning, Tim woke me up to get ready for church. I told him that I wasn't going to go to church. He said that I needed to get up and get ready or we would be late, later than usual. Again, I told him that I wasn't going to go to church. "How can I go to church and worship God when He doesn't care about me?" He said again that I needed to get ready for church. In frustration, I told him, "Well, I am only going to church because the Bible says that I am to be submissive to you (Ephesians 5:22-24 (NIV) "Wives submit yourselves to your own husbands as you do to the Lord. For the husband is the head of the wife as Christ is the head of the church, his body, of which He is the Savior. Now as the church submits to Christ, so also wives should submit to their husbands in everything", not because I want to."

He said, "Well, good, whatever it takes.

"Ugh", I thought. I begrudgingly got ready. On the drive to church, my arms were folded in front of me and I didn't have any expression on my face. When we arrived at church, I just walked in and sat down, arms still folded in front of me. This wasn't the typical me. I would usually be seen with a confident smile and I would be welcoming everyone around me. Not this Sunday was that going to happen. No way! I was not going to have joy this day, or so I thought. I can't tell you what the sermon was on that day, but I can tell you that God did a work in my life. At one point, close to the altar call, I silently talked to God. I said to Him, "Why did You not keep me safe? Why did You let those evil men hurt me? Why did You not love me enough to protect me??"

Suddenly I heard God in my heart of hearts, He whispered to me, "My sweet girl, remember what happened to My Son, Jesus? What would have happened if He was saved from dying on the cross?" Realizing that, I cried and made my way up to the altar. He was right. Jesus took on the sins of the world in a harsh way and then was nailed to a cross that He carried. After three days He became the Light of the World. As I knelt down at the altar, Pastor Dave met me there. He asked me why I came to the altar. I poured my heart out to him and shared all of those hidden memories and my hardened heart towards God. When I concluded, Pastor Dave sat with me on the steps of the altar and cradled me like a daddy would his beloved daughter. As he cradled me in his arms he told me how sorry he was that those harsh things had happened to me. Something extraordinary happened that morning. I realized that this deep dark secret that had been hidden deep inside of me was now exposed to the light therefore it couldn't harm me anymore. I am still guarded when I celebrate my birthday, but now I have joy in celebrating it too.

Chapter 14

HONORING UNCLE JOE

Uncle Joe's health was deteriorating seemingly rapidly. Because he was bedridden, he needed us to run errands for him quite often. The two things that I told him I could not or would not buy for him were alcohol and cigarettes. He understood, but wasn't happy about it. Oftentimes we would clean his house for him, but it was hard to stay on top of. Uncle Joe had a neighbor that would bring him meals and visit him. He enjoyed that. He also had an in-home support person who would come to his house and care for the bed wounds that he would get often and care for his diabetes, etc. She went above and beyond what her job entailed and would even run errands for him and grocery shop for him. He made frequent trips to the hospital. He had congestive heart failure and a few times he had pneumonia. There were several occasions that we were told his life was ending, but thank God, he would get better. We know he was a difficult patient. His constant back pain, phantom pains and bed sores were agonizing for him and because he was a heavy drinker and had a dependency for pain pills his aggressiveness increased. I felt bad for him. He didn't have to tell me that he was in pain, I could see it in him.

Because he was a difficult patient, I decided to call the hospital emergency room after each time Uncle Joe had been seen by them to thank them for caring for him.

One day, he told Tim and I that he was going to lose his house because he owed back taxes on it and couldn't pay the fees to keep it. We thought we would pull together with Ginger and Joey and try to help him, but he told us firmly that he didn't want us to do that. He explained that his health was getting worse and he was going to move into a guest home. I cried. He said that his health was not getting any better and instead of having to be put in an ambulance every couple of weeks and then having to go to the hospital and to a reha-bilitation hospital, it would be best for everyone if he just resided in one. He sold the house to the family that was bringing him meals. They paid the taxes on the house and then it was theirs. Uncle Joe gave many of his belongings away, but for the most part, the house and all of what was in the house now belonged to the new owners. Misty, Uncle Joe's dog was given to Uncle Rick. When Uncle Rick went to visit Uncle Joe at the rehabilitation hospital that he resided in, he brought Misty with him. I don't know who was more thrilled to see each other, Uncle Joe or Misty.

We visited Uncle Joe every Saturday. He loved seeing Nathaniel and Allison. He also loved us to wheel him out on the grounds in his wheelchair and take in the fresh air. He made many friends there. He made the best out of living there. He made sure that he had a big bag of dum-dum lollipops sitting right near him while he sat in his wheelchair. He would tell people that he had a treat for them, if they would smile for him. After he saw their smile, he handed them a dum-dum sucker. Everyone loved them! Hanging on the left arm of his wheelchair was a plastic grocery bag and on the other arm of the wheelchair dangled a grabber tool. About three to five times a day he wheeled himself around the grounds and picked all of the cigarette butts off the ground, put them in the grocery bag and threw them away. He said that doing that made him feel good. The maintenance people liked that he did this. This gave Uncle Joe a sense of accomplishment.

One Friday afternoon, when I called Uncle Joe on the cellphone that he had, he didn't answer. It wasn't like him not to answer. We talked almost every day and I knew that he wasn't feeling well lately. I had learned that if he didn't answer his phone, I should call the hospital. That is where he was. He was in the ICU on a breathing machine and he was in a coma. I knew that he would bounce back, he always did. We prayed with him and talked to him. I kept in close contact with the hospital. We saw him every day. On Monday, we were told that we needed to make some decisions. Uncle Joe had already named me as his decision maker on his advanced medical directive, however I didn't think that I could emotionally make his medical decisions for him. I called on God for His help! We had to make a decision on whether or not to have him moved to the Hospice House. I struggled with this. We talked for what seems like hours to the hospital workers and counselors. I was told that Uncle Joe wouldn't have to be in pain anymore. Hospice would have him be as comfortable as he could be. I told them that I didn't want him to die. I tried to hold back the tears. They said that not all people pass away there, some people get better. I still didn't know what to do. God graced me with Uncle Joe being able to wake up and talk to me. As hard as it was, I brought this up to him. He was weak. When I mentioned Hospice House, he became very quiet. I knew why. I took a breath and told him that he would be as comfortable as he could be and that when he was in pain, it would be addressed right away. He had told me that at the rehab, if he was in pain, because he was in the room at the end of the hall, he would always get his medication when they reached him, not when he was scheduled to have it. Hearing that he would have his medications right when he needed them caught his attention. He wanted to know though, if he did get better, would he be able to return to his *home*? I told him that we would check into that for him. When we brought that question up to the Social Worker on Uncle Joe's case, we were told that yes, he would be able to go back to rehab if he got better. I hurriedly told Uncle Joe and then it was decided that he would go to the nearby Hospice House. After about a day or so, Uncle Joe was taken to Hospice House. It was absolutely beautiful there. So many flowers, a waterfall, grass surrounding the house and the inside was so comfortable. Uncle Joe liked it there. He said the food and the company was good. I wondered if he was getting better, but his cough was still pretty bad and now he was on an oxygen machine. The day after Uncle Joe was moved to Hospice, we received a call from his case worker. He told us that he was sorry, but he found out that Uncle Joe would NOT be able to move back into the rehab if he got better. He said doing that was against policy and because he was new, he didn't know that. I was crushed! How was I ever going to tell Uncle Joe this? I was angry that I had given Uncle Joe false hope.

Our visits with Uncle Joe were nice. His mind was clear. He asked us about work, church, and God. He asked us to pray with him and we did. Many times he told me that he was proud of me and that he was so happy that I had Tim in my life and that he had us both in his life. He smiled a lot. On Friday night, Uncle Joe was quiet. Before we left, we prayed with him. When I kissed his cheek a tear fell from his eye and he smiled. As we were walking out of his room, I noticed a radio on his dresser and we put it on a Christian radio station.

Early the next morning, Hospice called our house. Tim answered the telephone. They said that Uncle Joe was declining and that we needed to get there as soon as we could. I showered as quickly as I could and we went to Hospice House. Uncle Joe passed away a few minutes before we arrived there. I felt like I let him down. I cried my eyes out. One of the nurses came over to me and tried to comfort me. She didn't try to stop me from crying, she was just right there with me. After I composed myself, she told me that she had told my "*dad*" that she was going to call me and ask me to come visit. She explained that some patients, after being told that, they don't want their family to watch them pass away. She went on to say that they don't want their loved ones' last memory of them to be them passing away, so they pass away before they get there. For some odd reason that made sense to me. I stayed with him and caressed his arm and his brow and laid my head against his arm. My tears drenched his arm. We had kept Ginger and Joey updated, but now I needed to call them and tell them that their dad was gone. That was hard. Ginger cried and Joey thanked me for calling and said that he was on his way. He lived about an hour and a half away. Ginger lived in another state, so she wouldn't be coming. The next call that I had to make was to Auntie Verla. I heard her heart break. She couldn't believe that she had now lost both Aunt Linda and Uncle Joe. She told me that she wanted Uncle Joe's ashes laid on top of her husband's grave. She said that she had already arranged it and talked to Uncle Joe about it. That is what we did. He is buried in Alameda, California amongst beautiful trees on a hilltop. He was laid to rest with his Uncle Cleo and one day Auntie Verla would join him in the grave-side that was reserved for her, right next to her husband. That day came three years later, when Auntie Verla made her way to heaven.

I felt such a huge emptiness without Aunt Linda, Uncle Joe and Auntie Verla in my life, but I also thanked God for all of the ways that each of them had invested in my life and the impact that they had on my life.

Chapter 15

GOD IS OUR PROVIDER

Tim and I have listened to a local Christian radio station–KAMB 101.5 Celebration Radio since soon after we met. There was once a program that they featured that really ministered to us in our finances. The late Larry Burkett did an afternoon question and answer radio show called *Money Matters*. He gave biblical counsel on personal finances. Although there were many things we learned through him, some points that have really stuck with us throughout our marriage is the importance of tithing to God and giving, saving and making additional payments to the principal balance of any loan, but especially our mortgage each month, or whenever possible. When we put this to practice, it may have been as low as $10.00 a month, but we did it. If we received a bonus or at tax time received money back, we would put more towards the principal payment. When we received money from Aunt Linda's estate, after tithing, we put a larger quantity of money into it. Doing all this at first didn't look like it was doing much, but after looking at it over a few months at a time you could see the mortgage shrinking. You see, when you pay the principal down early, you can possibly save tens of thousands in interest. We were able to pay off our 30-year mortgage in 11 years. What a good feeling that was! It brought us such freedom. God has been so faithful to us.

Tim and I had always hoped to have rental property for two reasons. One reason was to return the blessing of providing a home for a family at a rate that was lower than the market value. And two, because we were receiving adoption assistance funds and knew that one day it would come to an end, so we wanted to try and find a way to try and replace that income. We began looking at houses and had a Realtor working with us. After much prayer, we decided to purchase another home and rent out the one that we lived in. House prices were very low at this time. I loved our house that we were in and our entire neighborhood. I reluctantly joined Tim and our Realtor in looking at houses. Because we wouldn't go over the amount we thought we could feasibly afford our selection of houses wasn't very appealing. Some of the houses we looked at had very bright colored walls, some had holes in walls and doors, windows were knocked out and some were not in safe neighborhoods. We looked off and on for about a year and a half. Tim liked some of the houses, only because he has been blessed with the ability to see the *finished picture*, after all of the work would be done on the houses. All I could see was all of the work that needed to be done. Often through email, houses would be brought to our attention.

There was one house that caught my attention. It was a two story with a large living room that faced the front yard. That was a must for me. Before, when we bought our first home, I was adamant about wanting the living room that faced the front yard. Tim didn't have a preference and didn't mind that I kept my preference. We called our Realtor about the two story house and he was quick to tell us that we would get outbid. Tim and I were disappointed. The next day, Tim talked to another Realtor that we had talked to a few times earlier and he said the same thing, we were not going to get the house. But, as he and I looked at the numbers, it looked like that it was almost within our budget. We prayed and asked God what we should do. We still wanted to see it, so the next day we went and looked at it. It was two minutes from our house that we were living in. I loved it. It faced an open street and it was well kept. We noticed a paper on the door with a listing agent on it. We decided to call them and they happened to be about ten minutes away. We were told that someone would be there to let us in. When we went into the house, it was spacious and inviting. We looked through it and asked the Realtor who was with us what she thought our chances would be of having a successful bid. She told us that we wouldn't know unless we tried. After praying about it, we put in an offer and within a week we were told that our bid was one of the highest bids, but we had to increase it, if we wanted to get the house. Our original bid was $149,000. She wanted us to go into the low $150,000's, but we told her that we set a budget of $150,000 and that we weren't going to go over that. She said, "Well, come on, go to $151,000 at least." We reluctantly agreed. A few days later, we were told that we had the winning bid. We were both shocked and surprised. Now we had to think about packing. It was October, the kids were still in school and Donny and his family had planned to come to our home for a visit in November. I was now feeling stressed about it all. I realized that God had walked us through each step, He surely wasn't going to abandon us now. I decided to take a deep breath and trust Him! When we did the walk through, there were a couple of things that we were concerned about. Throughout the upstairs, there were many squeaks in the floor and the window on the roof revealed a leak, after an unexpected rain occurred. We mentioned these concerns to our Realtor. She said that normally foreclosed homes were sold *as is* and whatever repairs needed to be done the new owners would be responsible for. "But", she said, "It won't hurt to ask, the worse they can say is no." She submitted our concerns and within a few days we were told that everything would be repaired before we moved in. We weren't going to have to pay for any of it. God worked it all out for us. Now we hoped that we could find trustworthy tenants for our other home.

God came through for us again. We knew a family that was going to lose their home. They came on hard times and had a health crisis in their family. They were a family of four. We asked them if they would be interested in renting our home. They were surprised that we would offer. We already knew that these were very good people who just came on some hard times. We also knew that after being foreclosed on, it would possibly be hard for them to find a place to rent. They were interested in renting from us.

Everything seemed to happen fast. By November we were moved into our new house. We then readied the other house for its new home dwellers. Donny and his family came for a few days. It was so good to see them. Our new home wasn't completely put together yet, but his family understood and even helped us move things around. We were now getting settled into our new home. Three months later, in February the renters were able to move into the house we rented out.

I think that if we are diligent, we can see God working in our lives. One day out of the blue when I had been going through a tough time with my health and with the ups and downs of being a mom, while I was at work and it was recess time, I was unlocking the bikes when I felt something on my outer left arm near my shoulder. I was about to yell out because of my fear of spiders, but remembered that I had preschool children around me and I didn't want to scare them. I took a deep breath and looked over at my arm ever so carefully when I saw a beautiful butterfly trickling its wings on me. My heart fluttered as I said, "Awe, Thank you so much God!" A three-year old little girl, Daphne asked me what I was thanking God for. I told her that I just received a kiss from God because a butterfly was on my arm. She smiled and told me that that was nice of God to do that. Two years later Daphne, now five-years old was leading the class on a walk on the school grounds. At one point she asked, "Mrs. Patti, how come the sun is out but it is still so chilly?" I responded, "Well, Daphne, let's not focus on the chilliness, but on the sun." I then sang out, "*Mr. Sun, Sun, Mr Golden Sun, please shine down on me.*" Daphne blessed me when she replied,"Mrs.Patti, you always shine so brightly. You are like a kiss from God." This brought tears to my eyes. God used this little girl to speak hope into my life. I again thanked God for His goodness and grace.

I find that we often miss the little blessings around us when we choose not to slow down and pay attention. I strongly believe that no matter what hardships we may find ourselves going through, we need to do our best to stay positive. Sometimes we often blame God for the difficulties we go through when all along the difficulties we often go through are our own fault. Our actions can take a toll on us and the people around us whether they are positive or negative actions.

I often hear the phrase, "Is your cup half full or half empty?' I choose to be thankful to even have a cup. Some people don't even have that, it is up to me how filled up or how empty my cup is.

As a preschool teacher, I often hear the children say what they *can't* do. I try to encourage them to focus more on what they *can* do. There is always something that we *can* do if we spend more time focused on what we can do.

What helped me to have brighter days is how I decided to greet the preschoolers and their parents each morning when they came into preschool.

I came up with a new greeting with every day of the week. Sometimes I would change up the greeting determined by the weather or a holiday or a special event that we would have for a certain day. For the most part they went like this- 1) "Welcome to a Magnificent, Marvelous Miraculous Monday." 2) "Welcome to a Totally, Tremendously, Terrific Tuesday." 3) Welcome to a Wonderful, Wacky, Whimsical Wednesday." 4) "Welcome to a Thoroughly, Thoughtful and Thankful, Thinking of you Thursday." 5) "Welcome to a Fabulously, Fantastic, Funtastic, Faithful and Friendly Friday." Both the children and their families were tickled by the greetings that were shared with them each morning. But the smiles that came to me as I greeted them with those words blessed me more than the children could ever know!

Chapter 16

RAISING TEENAGERS AND ANOTHER DIAGNOSIS

W e had so much fun being Nathaniel and Allison's parents. We enjoyed everyday things with them like watching tv shows, going for drives or just being at home. A couple of things come to mind as I remember those times.

One December I was in my office area wrapping Christmas presents while nine-year old Nathaniel was outdoors playing with friends. At one point, Nathaniel came into the house calling for me. I hurriedly set everything aside and made my way to where he was. Nathaniel asked me what I had been doing. I told him that I was working on some things (I didn't want him to know that his gifts were being wrapped). Curious, he persisted on asking-inging me what things I was working on. I told him it was a secret. That caught his attention even more. Quick thinking got to me. "Well", I said, "there is something you don't know about me." He wondered what my secret could be. I went on to tell him that I was upstairs wrapping. A shocked look came across his face. "You know how to rap?", he asked. I told him that I sure did and that at once I had been a professional wrapper. He couldn't believe this. He asked me if I could rap for his friends. I told him that that would be too embarrassing for me to do. After he did some begging, I explained that I would need to gather all of my things and it could take awhile. He said that he would go get his friends and be back soon. I had to do some more quick thinking. I went into the garage and got a box then went into my office and put wrapping paper, ribbon, scissors, tape, tissue paper, a small box and gift bags into the box. I went into the living room and set my box on the coffee table and laid everything out. When Nathaniel brought his friends into the house, he looked confused and asked what I was doing. I said, "Well, you wanted me to show you and your friends how I wrap, so I'm going to show you." I then began to wrap a box. Nathaniel couldn't believe that he had been had. I felt pretty happy with myself for thinking that up in the spur of the moment.

One day while Nathaniel (10 years-old) and Allison (nine-years old) were playing in the backyard and I was making dinner, I could hear them talking as they were playing with some discarded wood that we had and some pvc pipes. After a few minutes my mind was on the music I had been listening to. Suddenly Nathaniel darted into the house with Allison following after him, yelling, "You told me to do it!" I asked her to stop talking so I could hear what Nathaniel had to say. When he opened his mouth to talk, all that came out of his mouth were not words, but bubbles. For some reason Nathaniel had dared Allison to pour bubble solution down a pvc pipe and try and make it into his mouth. Little did he know when he gulped it down, she was going to pour half of the bottle down the pvc pipe. We still laugh when we think of that day and I don't think that Nathaniel looks at bottles of bubbles quite the way anyone else does.

Many times neighbors would stop by because they thought that Nathaniel and Allison were fighting in the front yard. They were worried that one of them was going to get hurt. They were just wrestling with each other and having fun doing it. We decided that the best place for them to wrestle would be in the backyard.

As a family, we enjoyed going to amusement parks, the lake, the beach and all of their many sporting events.

Nathaniel and Allison loved sports. Nathaniel was involved in taekwondo, gymnastics, baseball, dance (for a bit), swim, wrestling, football and soccer. His pro sports were wrestling and soccer!

No matter what sport Nathaniel did, he was a huge achiever. He began swim lessons when he was five-years old. At one point he was asked to jump into the swimming pool by jumping off from the diving board. Nathaniel climbed the ladder and when he reached the top of the diving board, he made a run for the water and with the lifeguards yelling for him not to run, he did a flip off of the diving board and swam to the lifeguard that was in the pool. Everyone who saw the flip cheered for Nathaniel. When he came out of the pool, the head lifeguard explained to him that what he did was not allowed however if he came early the next day of practice he would love to videotape him doing it again. Another time, Nathaniel shocked a group of onlookers when he went to his first base-ball practice at 5-years old. As he walked up, the coach was doing a bit of heckling and directed all of the players to step in because "this little tyke wouldn't be able to hit the ball very far." Nathaniel picked up the bat and when the pitch was thrown, he hit that ball just right and everyone lifted their heads to follow the ball as it made its way over the faraway fence. They cheered for him in utter amazement. Because Nathaniel was not as big as the other kids and was mistaken for being younger than he was, he would often be underestimated. This gave him motivation to excel people's view of him. As a teenager, that didn't change. He proved himself over and over again by either scoring the winning pin in wrestling as he was wrestling the last match of the night, causing his school to achieve the lead championship or being the lead scorer on his school soccer team. Allison enjoyed taekwondo, gymnastics, softball, dance (for a bit), basketball for school and travel basketball and volleyball. Her pro sport was basketball! She was so gifted in that sport. She could dribble with both her left hand and her right hand and she could play any position. In a cross town 6th grade neck in neck playoff game, the clock was down to .38 seconds. The other team was ahead by one point. Alison made a judgement call opposite of what the coach had directed. Thankfully, that play allowed Allison to score the winning points, allowing the team to move onto the championship. The crowd cheered and although her coach gave her a talking to, he cheered for her too.

For three years, Allison was on a travel summer basketball team. That took us traveling on the weekends, which was nice because we could enjoy family time between games by exploring the towns that we were in.

I loved watching Nathaniel and Allison play their sports and both Tim and I loved rooting them on!

In Allison's sophomore year of high school is when sports ended for her. She had been on a volleyball team when she told me that she hadn't been feeling well. She thought it was food poisoning or maybe she had eaten too many marshmallows at a youth group competition, after all she did win the competition. She pushed and pushed herself to play in her volleyball games and she was awesome. I had a nudging feeling in me at work one morning and texted Allison and asked her how she was feeling. She had never missed school and this day she had called Tim at work from school and said she was sick. He picked her up and took her home. She texted me back that she thought she was dying and asked me to come home. Thankfully, I was able to leave work early. When I went into the house and saw her, she looked pretty bad. Every move she made hurt. She couldn't eat and couldn't sleep. I decided to take her to Urgent Care. Tests revealed that her appendix had ruptured 5 days prior. They said it was a miracle that she was alive. She was admitted into the hospital until her blood counts stabilized. I stayed with her. It was a scary time. Tim and I spent a lot of time in prayer, asking God to heal her and thanking God for helping her to stay strong.

In the midst of that going on, we had some added drama going on in our family. Nathaniel decided to make some choices that got him into trouble. At 15 years old he would disappear for days at a time. He was getting into fights, hanging out with people we didn't know and was being sucked into a wayward life. He already had trouble focusing in school and although he was a very giving person, he also wanted what others had. He dropped out of soccer and was barely ever home. He already had run away two different times because he had been grounded for being suspended from school. There were times when he would be home in time for dinner, but would keep his head leaning downward and he wouldn't look at us or talk to us. On one of those nights, his face had a cut on it and his cheek had a bruise and the knuckles on his right hand were bruised. When we asked him about it, he said that it wasn't any of our business. I yelled that it was our business. "We never know where you are, who you are with or if you are even going to make it home." Him being quiet angered me more. Tim was better at talking to him than I was, but sometimes there was just no reasoning with him at all.

Every year since our Pastor, Pastor Adam had Pastored at Ceres Christian Church he taught a nine-month *Theoddesey* class. It is somewhat like a college course. It takes a lot of discipline and determination to stay committed to it. It is grueling. It takes you through the journey and battleground of your entire life and helps you to face things and situations and even people that have shaped you into the person that you are. Yes, that means facing the demons from your past and the hurts, abuse, etc. For three years I thought about taking this class. And for three years I made many excuses as to why I couldn't take the class. Excuses that seemed acceptable to me. My kids sporting events (the class was held on Tuesday evenings and all of Nathaniel and Allison's games were held on Tuesdays and Thursdays.) I also did a lot of my planning for my preschool class on Tuesday's. Finally, one year I decided to make a list of all the reasons that I *could* take this class. It would make me a better wife, a better mom, a better friend, a better child of God. It would make me a better employee, a better teacher, a better co-worker, a better me. I decided that that list far outweighed the *why I couldn't* list, so I signed up. The class was to start in two weeks and I was getting fidgety about it. I was also having second thoughts about going. I thought about my diabetes. "What if I had an insulin reaction and no one would know what to do?", I told myself. I then realized that I was making yet another excuse for not taking the class. I told myself, "Okay, so what if I do have an insulin reaction? What could I do about that? Oh, I could have the people in the class know about my diabetes and then also let them know that I carry juice with me at all times in case I did have an insulin reaction." Problem solved. I was ready.

The evening of the class came and I was side-tracked by Nathaniel running away. We had no idea where he was. He didn't come home from school. I was upset. I had a decision to make. Was I going to let Nathaniel's actions prevent me from going to that first *Theoddesey* class (and if I let that happen, I knew that I wouldn't want to go the next week either) or was I going to pick myself up and go? Tim helped me with my decision. He explained to me that nothing I did was going to change what was going on. I decided that he was right and I went to the class. As I drove to my church, I prayed. I asked God to please give me His strength and endurance. When I was about a block from the church, I saw Nathaniel. He saw me too. He tilted his head at me with an odd smile. I drove on ahead and made my way to the class-room. The room was full. I was shaking, both from nerves and from frustration. Pastor Adam gave everyone an introduction to the *Theoddesey* class and then asked if anyone had any questions or comments. My heart was beating rapidly when I held up my hand. When he called on me I told him that I needed to make everyone aware of some-thing about me. I explained that I needed everyone to know that I have type 1 diabetes and that there may be times that my blood sugar drops, and if it does they might see me being quiet, edgy, shaky, sweaty, confused. I explained that if they saw me acting any of those ways not to ask me if I was okay. I gave them all permission to go into a small bag that I carry and take out the juice and hand it to me and tell me to drink it. They all agreed to do so. I felt such a relief when I saw that they understood. I felt a sense of freedom. I was ready to move forward.

The class had about twenty people when it started, but ended with just five of us, including Pastor Adam. I don't think it was because of what was taught that people dropped out, but due to the core of emotions that were being exposed. It was scary and it was time consuming. Each day, we read chapters and filled out blanks and revealed parts of ourselves on paper. We also were asked to spend fifteen minutes each day in complete silence, without any distractions. The idea was to think about how I was feeling, just one word and write it down on an index card. I chose to spend my fifteen minutes of silence, while the kids were at school and while Tim was at work, in my large walk-in closet, closed off from my cat and any noises that were going on around the outside of my house, it was hard. At first, I would think about all of the things that I should be doing- the laundry that I happened to be sitting near, the cleaning that needed to be done, etc. It took about three weeks for me to be able to completely clear my mind. Another phase of the class was in quiet time, we were asked to write down how we were feeling AND how we were going to choose to feel. Writing it down was much easier than following through with what I chose to feel. In those quiet times "*to do*" things would often creep into my mind. I decided to do what Pastor Adam had suggested, keep a tablet and pen close by and write those thoughts down when they came. After my quiet time, I could address what I wrote down. This made it easier to do my quiet time. It took a lot of discipline. I did a lot of soul searching. One thing in particular that came to my mind oddly enough was about my mom. I realized that if my mom had not had cancer, she would not have been admitted into a hospital and a Pastor would not be doing his rounds and would not have been able to minister to my mom and lead her in the sinner's prayer, paving her way to heaven. Ken would not have ever allowed a Pastor into our home or our lives therefore my mom wouldn't have known about the Saving Grace of God. So, you see, Ken didn't win, the enemy didn't win. I came to the realization that cancer had saved my mom's life.

During my quiet times, as you can imagine, I felt an array of feelings. There were many times that I had to convince myself to feel anything positive about myself, because I felt like a complete failure. Nathaniel was still often disappearing and I found out that he was telling stories about me to other people. Things like I wasn't feeding him or letting him into the house to sleep. He also told another story of me being very sick. Some of the stories were partially true, like being ill, but the other stories were exaggerated. At one point, a school counselor came to our house to see if something was going on. He saw that things were not as Nathaniel had said. A school police officer also came to our house, but didn't see any evidence of what people had heard Nathaniel say at the school to be true.

Tim and I did our best to go to every sporting event that Nathaniel and Allison were in. We loved cheering them on. Due to Tim's work schedule, he would get to their games about 30 minutes late, but I was blessed to have a work schedule that allowed me to be early to their games. There were a few times that when I walked into the school gym to watch Allison's basketball games and as I made my way to a bleacher seat I would hear whispering, "*That's* Nathaniel Robinson's mom", and then there would be an uncomfortable hush and stares as I sat down.

While going through the *Theyoddessey* class God spoke to my heart. The most important and most powerful thing that I learned is that I am a beloved child of God. Me! I Am A Beloved Child of

God! I never felt like I was anyone's beloved child. It took me a couple of weeks to be able to say those words out loud. Hearing those words and saying them for the first time caused me to weep. Knowing this truth gave me a new perspective. I felt that now instead of living in a black and white world (that I now recognized it to be), I was now living my life in full color. God was doing a new thing in me.

A powerful lesson came in the lesson on forgiveness when Pastor Adam said that it was important for us to forgive those who have done harm to us, "any kind of harm", he emphasized. This was troublesome to me because I thought forgiving meant that the person that needed to be forgiven did nothing wrong if I forgave them. It was explained to me that forgiveness is for our individual selves. Forgiveness causes what was done to us to not take up space in our brain or in our hearts anymore. Unforgiveness can hold us captive. How I came to grips with it was realizing that me thinking about the abuse was letting the abusers win. I decided that I couldn't let that happen. I also decided that my childhood was stolen from me and that Bob, Ken and the evil one and his lies were not going to take my adulthood away. I have to work hard at remembering this. I have chosen to forgive both Bob and Ken. Not for them, but for me! I have even tried to find them to confront them and let them know that neither of them had power over me however they were nowhere to be found.

Another thing that I felt that God was telling me to do was to stop allowing Nathaniel's actions to name who I was, but instead allow God to name who I am. This was hard to do, but I asked God to help me with this. At the next basketball game that Allison played at her school gym, I mustered up the courage to face the people who were making harsh comments about me *being Nathaniel's mom*. When I heard those words, I stopped walking and I looked up at them. I then waved at them and said, "Hi, that's me, I'm Patti Robinson, I'm here to root our team on. I will be sitting over there." I pointed over to the area I would be sitting and said, "You are welcome to join me over there and root the team on with me, or not." And I went and sat down. It was hard to do, but once I did it, I don't recall if anymore comments were ever made, or if I just didn't pay any attention to them anymore.

Nathaniel was always defensive when we asked him where he would be going or for how long he would be out. He often told us that where he went and what he did was none of our business. Tim and I talked together about what we should do about Nathaniel's disrespect and the choices that he was making and made the decision to set firmer boundaries. During one of Nathaniel's unreasonable outbursts, Tim let him know what those boundaries were. He said, "If you want dinner each night, you need to be at the kitchen table no later than 7 pm If you want a nice warm bed to sleep in, then you need to be home by curfew." Now that Tim said this, we both knew that knew that we would need to follow through with it.

Because Nathaniel was regularly skipping school, Tim had told him that if he wanted to live with us that he needed to go to school. The next day he skipped school again. When he came to the house in the evening, Tim told him that because he didn't go to school, he wasn't going to live in our home. He then asked if he could sleep in the backyard. Tim agreed. There were a few nights at about 2 am, I would hear coughing on the side of the house. It was Nathaniel. I cried. Tim and I had to do our best not to *rescue* him. But, let me tell you, it was so hard to do!

God revealed four words to me in the last part of my *Theoddessey* journey I was on. The words were "Respond, Do Not React!" Another hard thing to do. I was confident that there were going to be countless situations that were going to come up that I would have to try to practice this new goal of 'responding and not reacting'.

During the time that I was in the *Theoddesey* class, Nathaniel was continuously making way-ward choices and disappearing for days at a time.

After praying about what to do and after talking to Tim about all of the despair that was going on in our family, I decided to write down all of the food banks and shelters in our area and the addresses and times that they gave out food and offered shelter. The day I wrote this list out, Nathaniel had been home for a couple of days. That day, he came down the stairs with his backpack on and asked me if I wanted to know where he was going. I said, "Sure." He explained that he was going to the police station to let them know that we weren't feeding him or letting him sleep in his bed and that they would need to find him a new home. I told him that I needed to tell him something. He looked at me and told me that if I wanted to tell him something then it would need to be fast. He looked down at his watch, then said that I had 45 seconds to tell him what I needed to say. I walked away.

He said, "Aren't you going to say something?"

I said, "Well, if what I have to say isn't important for you to hear, then it's not important for me to say." He then wanted to know what I had to say. I told him, "Nathaniel, I love you. I care about you and so does God. Since you are packed and ready to go, I thought you would need this list. It is a list of all of the food banks and shelters that are available and the times that they are available. I pray for you everyday and Nathaniel, and I always will.

I also need you to know that I believe in you and I believe that God has a plan for you."

He said, "Okay, bye", and he was gone. I felt like such a failure. A horrible mom is what I felt I was. Then I wondered if I was going to be in trouble? Did I break the law? Was I going to be arrested? So many things went through my mind. I sat on the couch and decided that I was going to beat Nathaniel at his own game and call the police on myself. So, I did. I called them and told them that I would like to turn myself in.

"Who is this?" I was asked.

"My name is Patti Robinson," I said. "Patti Robinson?" (They already knew who I was and who Tim was).

"What did *you* do?" I explained that Tim and I told our son (they were aware of who our son was) that if he wanted to have a warm meal to eat at dinner time, he would need to be home by 7 pm and if he wanted a nice warm bed to sleep in, he would need to be at home by the 10 pm curfew. The Officer I spoke with was quiet after I said what I said. I then asked him if they were going to come and get me or if I should drive to them. He chuckled and said, "Neither. You both told your son what he needed to do and he chose not to do what he needed to do. That was his choice. I am taking notes for myself—I might have to use this tactic myself." Whew! I didn't do anything wrong in the eyes of the law. That was a relief.

There were a couple of times that an Officer would ask me about things that Nathaniel had done and because I couldn't remember the details of the event, I decided to start a private prayer message group with trusted friends on Facebook. It became a safe haven for me. There were a few times that I was really scared of what Nathaniel might do and that prayer message board brought me an array of peace.

Something else that helped both Tim and I was that our friends Tom and Mel, who had gone through similar struggles with their adopted son became our much needed sounding board. They offered ideas and validation, something that I didn't realize I even needed. They were a huge support to us.

Tim and I tried hard to get help for Nathaniel. We tried counseling, but after about four sessions the counselor said that he couldn't help him. We looked to Social Services for help, but they said that there wasn't anything that they could do. We tried Military School, but he was kicked out. Even though Nathaniel had great mentors in his life which included several youth pastors and spon-sors as well as sport coaches, he had a glorified view of being a criminal. We were at our wits-end and pleaded with God daily for a miracle. Finally a miracle came when Nathaniel was arrested, after involving himself in some illegal activity. This began the process of us getting the help that we needed for him..

Tim went to Nathaniel's court date. The judge was going to release Nathaniel to us, on house arrest, but Tim requested that Nathaniel not be able to return to our home. He and I had already talked about this. I didn't feel safe with Nathaniel at home and we didn't trust him.

It put our minds at ease when the Judge decided that it would be in ours and Nathaniel's best interest to extend his stay in juvenile hall until a group home could be found for him.

In the midst of all of what was going on in our family, I was having some health issues. I suffered from mouth, throat and stomach ulcers, making it almost impossible to drink or eat anything. This was really hard on my diabetes. I tried every mouth sore medicine that I could, but nothing eased my pain. My white blood counts, red blood counts, platelet counts and other counts were all danger-ously low. I was seeing a hematologist and was told that this just might be *my new normal.* I knew that it wasn't. The tongue ulcers were holes that went almost all the way through my tongue. My energy was completely gone. I work about 20 minutes from where we live and I had to daily pull over from tiredness two times before arriving home. Doctor Zhou talked to me about possibly having a bone marrow biopsy, but decided because my blood work was clear that I didn't have cancer, a bone marrow biopsy wasn't needed and he didn't want to put me through that if it wasn't needed. He also talked to me about Neulasta injections that could help me. He said that the downfall to having the injection was that it was only a temporary fix that would last about three weeks and I would receive the injections every four weeks. He didn't feel that there was a need for me to receive them. We had a hard time accepting that this was just the way it was and that there was no treatment to treat what was going on in me.

After thinking about it more and realizing that my health wasn't getting any better, Tim and I decided to go to another doctor for a second opinion. The second doctor decided to do a bone marrow biopsy. After the test was done, this doctor also concluded that I did not have cancer and that there was no treatment for my condition. About 6 months later, we decided to request a referral for an appointment with UCSF (University of California at San Francisco) to see if they had any solutions for me. Of course, when we went, I didn't have any mouth ulcers. I am thankful that I thought to take a picture of the one that I had had just days prior to my appointment. Doctor Leavitt took down all of my information in great detail. He also had me get bloodwork done before we left that day. He said that he would talk to his team of doctors about my condition and then set me up with a new appointment three weeks from that day to have a bone marrow biopsy done. Another bone marrow biopsy? The first one really hurt, even after being numbed, I felt every turn of the doctor's hand as the needle went through my pelvic bone. God helped me through that one, so I knew that He was also going to help me with the second one. I didn't have any doubts about it!

Within two days, Doctor Leavitt called me to see how I was doing. He said that my blood work was dangerously low and he was concerned that if I got a bad infection, it could be dangerous for me. He changed my appointment for a week earlier than the original appointment.

The day before my appointment at UCSF, Nathaniel ran away. Tim took it pretty hard. He was trying to do everything he could to help me and now when it seemed that we were going to hopefully get some answers and solutions, this happened. After praying about it, because I was so ill and had a really bad tongue ulcer in the middle of my tongue about the size of a pencil eraser and two down my throat and because my weight was really down, we decided that we needed to go forward with the scheduled appointment. We knew through a school campus portal that Nathaniel was at school that day and we knew that Allison would be busy with basketball practice after school. We kept the appointment with UCSF and our friend, Bill, who was also one of our Pastors offered to pick up Nathaniel from school. UCSF is about 100 miles away from where we live and it takes about 3 hours to get there because of traffic. We dropped Allison off with our good friends Mike and Lisa at 5 am and then made our way to UCSF. When Doctor Leavitt looked at me he had a look of concern on his face. My weight was down to about 90 pounds. He could see that I was in a lot of pain. When he saw the ulcer on my tongue, he became alarmed. He decided that I needed to get a Neulasta injection as soon as possible. He told me that he didn't want me to go home until I had one however because he was unable to get our insurance to approve it, I went home without it.

Two weeks later, I had my second bone marrow biopsy. This one was much easier than the first one. The first one was done manually, the second one was done with a new technique using a drill. I know that it sounds painful, but it was much quicker and not as much pressure was used. The bone marrow biopsy revealed that my bone marrow was working fine, but antibodies inside my body were attacking and destroying my white blood cells. It was decided that monthly Neulasta injections were needed to improve the quality of my life. UCSF did the legwork to get the Neulasta approved by our insurance. Doctor Leavitt tried to get the approval before we left that day too, because he wanted to give me the injection before we left. That didn't happen. About three days later, he called and told me that he had talked with the insurance for 40 minutes and was finally able to get the okay. He said that because Neulasta injections are for people who are living with cancer and because I didn't have cancer, the insurance said that there was no need for me to have the injections. Doctor Leavitt explained to them that I have a condition called Pancytopenia, a reduction of all blood elements and asked them if they would rather face a wrongful death lawsuit because without the Neulasta injections I would die. Praise God, they saw the need for me to get them and they okayed the injections.

Due to the distance UCSF is, Doctor Leavitt was able to communicate with Doctor Zhou and have the Neulasta injections given to me at the medical center closer to my home. I was able to get the injection right away. The injections were cold and painful going in and for about a week after the injections, my bones were really sore. Every movement I made was difficult, but I managed. I had to get blood work done twice a week for about four months so they could chart my blood counts. Doctor Zhou once mentioned to me that about 67% of people with my condition don't do well with it. I decided right then to live like the 33% that do do well with this condition because living your life in a positive way is good medicine.

For a few months or so, I was still having mouth and throat ulcers. The awesome people at the Medical Center worked tirelessly on making new mouthwash rinses for me so I could try to eat. The best one that was created worked for only about 5 minutes. So after rinsing, I would try to eat as quickly as I could before the mouth pain would start back up. Within about 6 months, when I went in for blood work before my Neulasta injection, the nurses could tell the injections were working for me. They all said that I was looking healthier and had more color. It was then that they shared with me that they had thought that I was really going downhill since the first time they had seen me. I didn't realize how bad I was. When I went in for my Neulasta injections it was difficult emotionally, because it was where all of the people who were living with cancer were getting their treatments. I decided that I would try to encourage them and just be there to listen to them. They really blessed me by sharing their stories with me. I decided to always carry coconut oil that is in a tube with me and offer it to them to help them fight against the dry skin that chemotherapy causes.

Another health issue that was battled is cysts in my breasts. About two to three times a year since I was in my early 30's, they have been a common occurrence. I had a great doctor, Doctor Agbunag who would drain them right away each time. In 2014, I felt a rather large lump in my left breast. It really bothered me, so I called Doctor Agbunag right away. He did an ultrasound and decided it was a solid mass that would need to be surgically removed and sent off for testing. This surprised me because for years the lumps had always been liquid and easily drained. I trusted Doctor Agbunag. I knew I was in good hands. My faith was being tested though. Just as I thought that I was getting my health in order, this happens. I prayed and first thanked God for walking me through all of my battles and asked Him to continue to carry me through. I then said, "Lord, I would rather be ill in Your will than well and not in your will. This is Your story Lord, please walk me through this next journey we are on." In November, I had to go in for a breast biopsy. Doctor Agbunag did not do the biopsy, another doctor did, Doctor Trillo. When I walked into his office, I visited a bit with the nurse (whom I already knew because of previous appointments I had had there) and she prayed with me. She already knew about my faith, I was not at all shy about it. When Doctor Trillo came into the room, he introduced himself and asked me how I was doing and asked if I was ready. I told him that I was okay and that I was ready, because I knew that it was not his hands that would be working on me, but God's hands.

He said, "Well I think you need to know a little something about me. I was raised Seventh Day Adventist and for thirty years I have been agnostic."

"I'm sorry", I said, "now I know how to pray for you." He then told me that he would be working on me for about forty-five minutes and that would give me forty-five minutes to share with him what I believe and why I believe it. I gladly took on the challenge. After the forty-five minute biopsy and witness talk was done, Doctor Trillo took off his gloves and walked out of the room.

The nurse helped me up and as she bandaged me up she asked me, "How did you do that?"

"Do what?" I asked.

She said, "I have worked with him for over twenty-five years and he won't listen to anything I have to say about God and when anyone talks about God, he quickly changes the subject."

I smiled, "God must have had a plan for today." She told me that she was going to go out and see what she could find out about my biopsy.

When she came back she told me that Doctor Trillo was leaning against the hallway wall outside the room I was in and when she went up to him he told her, "That young lady sure did give me a lot to think about." My heart leapt for joy. God was using my battle to open the door for blessings. I was humbled.

December 26, 2014 was the day that Doctor Agbunag scheduled my lumpectomy. The first thing I had to do though was make sure my blood counts were in safe range. Whew, they were. The second thing I had to do was to get a marker placed in the lump. The marker was a long ten-inch wire. When the attending nurse tried to put the wire in, she had a hard time. It was so painful. After three tries, she apologized and asked me if I was okay. I said, "If my Lord can go through a crown of thorns and pierced hands and feet, then this is nothing", and I urged her to keep trying. She apologized for the pain that I was in and I told her I forgave her. It took her about five more tries, but she was finally able to get it done.

A nurse came in the room we were in and said, "The hospital thinks she went AWOL, what should I tell them?" "Tell them she is on her way", she told him. She carefully put my sweater around me and as quickly as Tim could, he escorted me to the car, then to the hospital. It was a cold December morning and putting a seatbelt on with that wire was almost unbearable, but we made it there and they were ready for me. I was taken back into the surgery area and put on a gurney. As I waited for Doctor Agbunag, Tim sat with me and so did his sister, Terry. I sure wanted that uncomfortable wire out. When Doctor Agbunag came in, he told me that he had two calls about me that morning. I couldn't imagine who would be calling about me. Tim was right there with me and so was Terry. He told me that the nurse who put the wire in me called to apologize for taking so long and she said that she felt really bad for hurting me. I told him that I already told her that I forgave her. He told me, with a smile that she mentioned that to him. I asked him who the other call was from. He said it was Doctor Trillo. I had a look of surprise.

"Why would he be calling about me?" I asked.

"He wanted to see how you were doing and wanted you to know that he was praying for you, and that he is reading his Bible." You can only imagine the elation I felt at that moment. I was so excited to know that. I realized that we never know what an impact our lives, no matter what we are going through, our encouraging words or even our health issues can have on others, *if* we allow it.

The biopsy result was that it was a pre-cancerous calcification and since it was removed, praise God there was no further concern.

After getting himself into some trouble, Nathaniel was arrested, he was to be in juvenile hall for about 90 days. It ended up being 60 days. It was really hard to visit him. Tim visited him every other weekend in that two-month period, I went twice. Nathaniel was pretty quiet during our visits, but he would talk. Tim has always had a good way of starting conversations and this skill was useful in a place like juvenile hall.

Something that I wish they would change about juvenile hall is having the parents pay the fees for their child to stay there. I personally feel like it should be the juvenile's responsibility to pay the fee. Perhaps doing community service until the fees are paid would be sufficient. We did every-thing we could think of to help prevent Nathaniel from taking the path that he was on. Now, we were going to have to pay for his juvenile hall stay.

Both Nathaniel and Allison had had a local paper route ever since they were 12 and 13 years old. Once a week they would deliver for the local newspaper and after they collected from the people they delivered the paper to, they were able to keep some of the money. When they turned the rest of the money back into the newspaper office, they were paid a bit more money. We had them do this so they could have their own spending money. We set up a system for the money. They both had three containers each. One container was for giving, one was for spending and the last one was for saving. Month to month, with tips they could collect $25-$40. They had their paper routes until Nathaniel was 15 years old and Allison stopped when she was 17 years old.

From early on, the money that we were receiving from the County for taking care of Nathaniel and Allison, we put a set amount of money each month in an account that we had opened for them. We hoped that the money would one day be used to help them pay for college or help them to put a down payment on a house. However, Nathaniel's account was dwindling, due to his indiscretions, because we always used the money that we had set aside for him to pay for the debts that he had incurred.

Another court date was set and at that court hearing, the Judge ordered for Nathaniel to be placed in a school for troubled teens outside of California. The problem with that though was the cost. This school for troubled teens was very expensive. Our County did cover a large portion of the cost, but they also required that Tim and I cover a portion of the cost, based on our income. We were told that Nathaniel's Medi-Cal was going to be canceled and that we would need to put him on our health insurance, which was another large expense. The County only accepts wage garnishment as a form of payment for child support. When

we adopted Nathaniel and Allison, we were assured
they would have Medi-Cal until they reached the
age of 18. We understood the amount of money
that we were required to pay, although we thought
that it was higher than it should have been, but we
just couldn't accept that the child support department could override the adoptions department and
take away the Medi-Cal. After spending much time
in prayer over this, we decided that we wanted to
get a hearing before a Judge. Soon after, we were
on our way to the courthouse to file the paperwork necessary to get a hearing and while walking
down the sidewalk of the courthouse, Tim looked
down at the two stacks of papers he was carrying
and said, "Oh no! These papers can't have staples
in them, they need to be paper clipped together."
We knew that we didn't have any paper clips with
us. We decided to pray about it right then. We
prayed that God would allow us to find two large
paper clips before we arrived at court. As hard as
it was, we told God that if we didn't have the two
paper clips, we would walk away and not go into
the courthouse. After praying, we took a few steps
and we found a large silver paperclip on the sidewalk. We thanked God for it and trusted that He
was with us. As we continued to make our way to
the courthouse, we scanned the sidewalk in hopes
of finding another one. When we reached the
steps, it looked like we were going to be walking

away from the doors of the courthouse, instead of through those doors. We continued up the stairs and when we made it to the second to the last step from the top, it was there that we found paperclip number two. That was just the confirmation that we prayed for and that we needed. I am curious at what the people who were around us thought when they saw our excitement at that moment as we thanked God.

While we were waiting for a court date to come, Tim kept thinking about the words of Jesus in Matthew 5:25 (NASB), "Make friends quickly with your opponent at law while you are with him on the way." Tim felt convicted by this verse. One week before the scheduled court date, Tim contacted the Child Support Department and told him that we would agree to all that they wanted, including the Medi-Cal insurance. They replied by saying, "It is too late, we are going to court." Through this, God gave both Tim and I, at separate times the exact same scripture from the Bible- Exodus 14:14 (NIV) "The Lord will fight for you, you need only to be still."

I was uncomfortable in the courtroom. The cases were parents taking each other to court for child support. Many of the cases were of a guy and a girl who had a brief dating relationship that resulted in a child being born. The mothers were suing for child support and the fathers didn't want to take any responsibility for the child. When Tim and I were called up, it was clear to the Judge that we weren't the typical case that he would see from day to day. We were holding hands and we were intact. When the Judge gave us our turn to speak, we mentioned that we did think that we should contribute to the cost of the group home that Nathaniel was in, however we just felt that the amount that we were being required to pay was a little high and we were requesting that it be reduced. Social Services had already agreed to reduce mine. We asked the Judge to take into consideration our medical expenses due to my health conditions. Both Tim and my wages were garnished by-weekly to help pay for the group home Nathaniel was in. It was hard, but God was so faithful to us through it all. After the Judge looked the medical expenses over, he decided to reduce Tim's portion of the child support. As far as the Medi-Cal, it was taken care of by Social Services and resulted in Nathaniel being allowed to stay on Medi-Cal. Praise God!

During the financial compromise, we were considering contacting our tenants and raising the monthly rent but we really didn't want to. We decided to pray about it. We also didn't want to limit our tithing to our church. God again, did something that completely shocked us. Our renters came to us and said, "We have something to tell you." Right away we thought that we were going to be told that they were giving us notice that they were going to be moving out. That's not what happened. Instead, we were told, "We've been waiting for you guys to raise the rent, but because you haven't, we decided to do it for you and we have included it in this months' rent." Ira then handed us the rent check. It exceeded what we were considering raising the rent to. Now, who does this? God does!

Allison was now in basketball season. She was a Sophomore in high school and she was at the height of the sport that she was most passionate about–basketball. She was so much fun to watch. She gave it her all and she wasn't afraid of anything! Every game, I was completely out of breath from cheering for her. I loved it! With all of this came something else though, something that I had feared for a long time. A complete interruption in my life. Something I had been so scared to face, but knew that one day, I would have to.

Ever since God allowed Tim and I to be the parents of Nathaniel and Allison, we were always honest with them about how we became a family. We kept it simple. We told them that there were two people who wanted to be parents, but couldn't and then there were two people who could birth kids, but were not equipped to be good parents. And with the help of God and our Social Worker angels, we became a family.

I know that I always had a hard time talking about Nathaniel and Allison's biological mom and biological dad, Diana and Mark-Paul. I felt like talking about them would make them miss them and maybe they wouldn't look at me as their mom anymore. Tim didn't mind talking to them about Diana and Mark-Paul. When he tucked in Nathaniel and Allison each night while they were growing up, they would all wrestle together and at times they would talk about them. I was okay with this, but it still made my heart hurt. Tim understood my feelings. And after he tucked the kids in, he very carefully shared with me what and who they had talked about.

As life went on, at times Allison brought up Diana and Mark-Paul. She knew that Mark-Paul was not available however she wondered when she would be able to meet Diana. This hit me like a ton of bricks, but I kept my composure. I told her that after she turns 18, if she still wanted to meet Diana, then the next day we would do that. She was okay with that.

On one particular day in October of 2014, I came home from work and there was a message on our answering machine. When I listened to the message, it was the kids Aunt Emily. She said,

"Hi Patti, this is Emily, I need you to call me immediately, I really need to talk to you." Emily usually called about two or three times a year over each year and we would schedule a time to meet with her with the kids. This call was different. I called her back and she told me that she needed me to know that Diana and Chris (Diana's brother) were contacting Allison. I asked her how she knew this and how they were doing this. She told me that they were contacting her through social media and that they were doing that as we spoke. Allison was at school during this time. I was angry because 1) Allison was being contacted during school and 2) Allison wasn't 18 yet. I thanked Emily for letting me know and then our conversation was over. Afterwards, as I paced in my living room, I asked God to help me process what was going on and to give me His divine wisdom and guidance. I must have done this for about forty-five minutes, because when I looked up at the clock it was 3:15. Allison had an away game and the school bus left the school for the away game at 2:15. I called Allison on her cell phone, but she didn't answer. I decided to call Diana. I had her number, because over the years she had called me two or three different times. She had wanted to know about the kids and wanted to meet them. I explained to her that that was up to them. If after they turned 18 and if they wanted to meet her then we would set it up.

This time when I called her and she picked up the phone I said, "Hi Diana, this is Patti."

She paused and then said, "Hi."

I continued, "I called to tell you that whatever trust we were building with each other is now gone. You went behind my back and contacted Allison and that was wrong!" There was another pause and I said, "I can see that our conversation is over, bye!" I hung up the phone. I then just sat down on the couch. I had to catch my breath. My brain was on fast forward. Tim wasn't due home for about an hour, so I tried calling Allison again and again, but there wasn't any answer. Finally, I decided to text her and ask her why she was not responding to me.

She texted me back asking, "Why did you cuss my mom out and threaten her??"

"Cuss her out?" I thought, "Threaten her? How? What was she talking about"? (I have never used any cuss words and I am not a threatening type of person.) I texted her back that that was not at all what had happened. No response. I couldn't wait for Tim to get home. I had so much to tell him. When he finally arrived home, he told me that he had something to tell me. He said that he had had an interesting day. ("*He* had an interesting day?" I thought, "he has no idea the day

I had.") He went on to tell me that his co-worker, Lisa who has a niece, who years ago had a child with Mark-Paul said that she thought he would want to know that she found out that Mark-Paul's fiance, Jamie had been in contact with Allison, as well as some other family members. We talked about that for a bit and then I told him what had transpired throughout my day. He was surprised. Again, we tried to call and text Allison. Still no response. Tim and I prayed and asked God, yet again for His wisdom and guidance.

The school bus was due back at the school by 9 pm. It looked like it was going to be a late night and Tim and I both got up each morning at about 4:45. I contacted our prayer group and asked them to please pray over our family. At about 8:30 pm, I was able to doze off. Tim woke me up at 8:45 and told me that he was going to go pick up Allison and we prayed together again. Remember what God told me to do earlier? "Respond, do not react'? This was a real challenge. When Tim left, I couldn't go back to sleep. Instead, I paced and prayed. I was getting really good at this. It was not a silent type of prayer. It was an outspoken type of prayer that included telling the devil to get behind us. 9:15 pm came and went. The school is only four minutes away from our house. When it became 9:30 pm, I decided to call Tim and ask him what was going on. My mind wanted to go places that I didn't want it to. I was relieved when Tim answered his phone very calmly. When I asked him where they were and if everything was okay, he said, "Everything is fine, we are just chatting at the park." His voice was calm.

"Thank You, Lord", I said as I looked up as if He was physically right there.

About 15 minutes later, both Tim and Allison walked into the house. I was waiting at the door. When Allison walked in, she gave me a hug and said that she was sorry. I hugged her back and told her that the whole day came as a surprise with all of the events that had happened. She said that she was sorry that she asked me why I cussed Diana out. Then she said, "After I thought about it, I realized that the only bad word I ever heard you say is, "Shut up", and that only a time or two."

"Whew", I thought.

Then she said, "And I know that you wouldn't have ever threatened to hurt Diana, because that's not you." I explained to Allison that I knew that this day was going to happen and I was afraid of it, because I thought it would mean that I would be losing her. I explained to her that if she would let me, I would love to be able to walk the journey with her. It was late and we had to get up for work early and she had to get some sleep before school the next day.

After Allison went to bed, I asked Tim what happened after he picked her up at the school. He told me that when she came to the car, she was a bit distant. As they drove off, he said, "I am really excited for you. You have wondered a long time about Diana and now you have been able to talk to her. What was it like?" He said that Allison's entire demeanor changed. (Another 'respond, do not react' action that proved to be positive.) I knew that I had a big decision to make. Either I was going to try and walk with Allison through this journey, or Allison was going to go behind our backs and do it on her own, without any support at all. Decision made. "Lord", I said, "if she will let me, I want to walk this journey with her and with You at our side."

I left for work each day early, before Allison got up. The next morning when I gathered my bag that I took to work with me each day, there was a letter on it, intricately folded and written by Allison. I wanted to read it right then but I had to leave for work, so I tucked the letter in my purse. God was good to me though, my usual trek to work takes about twenty minutes. On this day every light was green and the traffic was smooth. I was at work ten minutes early. I hurried in and read the letter. Tears streamed down my face as I read it. The letter read: "*Mom, I just want to thank you for everything that you have done, for taking care of me and making me laugh when you could tell that I was having a bad day. Thank you for being a woman of God, so that I can walk in your footsteps. Thank you for never giving up on me even though you may have felt like you wanted to. Most of all, thank you for loving me. Your love is unconditional. Your love is like a big teddy bear that I can squeeze when life gets tough. Thank you for believing in me in school, sports and just everything that gets thrown at me. Thanks for believing that I can get through it and I would love for you to walk this journey with me. I love you so, so much, no matter how things go, even if we fight or don't like what is going on, I will always love you. Forever and always. Love, Allison Robinson."* As my tears streamed out of my eyes, I thanked God for this moment. Thankfully, the children who normally came early were later than usual. This gave me time to freshen up my make-up.

When Tim came home from work, I couldn't wait for him to read the letter. He was happy that Allison reached out to me. I love writing letters and cards and it is rare that I get one, so it's really special for me when I do get one and Tim knows that about me. We prayed together and thanked God for working in this difficult situation and asked God to open the doors of communication for all of us. We stood on His promise found in Romans 8:28 (NASB) "And we know that

God causes all things to work together for good to those who love God, to those who are called according to His purpose."

Later that day, after Tim picked Allison up from practice and they came in the house, Allison gave me a big hug. I thanked her for the letter and told her that it meant so much to me and that I would always treasure it. She then opened up about a lot of things that Diana had been telling her. Diana made herself sound like a good person and said that it was she who was the victim when CPS came and removed Nathaniel and Allison from her home. Tim and I decided that if Allison wanted to go through all of the county papers and documents that we were given when she and Nathaniel came to us, then she could take them up to her room and go through them. When we suggested this, she decided to not go into her room and look through them, but stay in our room with us and read them, so that is what she did. We thought that this would be best because from what Diana had been telling Allison, it seemed that Social Services, CPS and the Police Department were all ganging up against her. After Allison read all of the paperwork, she was surprised by some of what she read and she came to the conclusion that Diana was not being truthful to her about what had happened.

Aunt Emily was curious about what was going on, so I called her. She decided that she wanted to come over to our house and talk in detail to Allison about what had transpired in those earlier days with both Diana and her brother, Mark-Paul. While she was at our house, she told Allison that she knew that her and Nathaniel were being well taken care of by being with us. She said that she could not have given them what they had been given by being with us. She also mentioned that some of the gifts that she and Nana had given to Nathaniel and Allison over the years had come from Mark-Paul. He would send whatever money that he would have and ask Emily and Nana to buy gifts for them. She then confirmed everything that was said in the county papers and she told Allison that if she had any questions about any-thing she could always ask her.

On Allison's 16th birthday Diana called and said that she wanted to get something off her chest. I said I would listen. She then told me that Nathaniel and Allison did not share the same father. She said that she had been made preg-nant by someone else and that the guy didn't know about this until recently. I was shocked at this news. I thought to myself that if it was true, then there is a man out there who has a son who was taken away by Child Protective Services and put in a foster home, then adopted out. This couldn't be true! I listened to everything that she had to say and then the phone call ended. Tim and I talked about this new revelation. Nathaniel resembled Mark-Paul to a tee. We pondered this for a time.

After a couple of weeks of praying for God's guidance, Tim and I decided to be open to the idea of us and Allison meeting Diana. She had a steady man in her life and had two boys with him. They were three and five. We met at a McDonald's restaurant. It was odd and a bit uncomfortable. I was still uncomfortable with Diana because of her earlier accusations and the lies that she told. Diana also seemed to be a bundle of nerves. Allison was a little nervous and Tim, he seemed to be at ease. Allison and Diana gave each other a short and seemingly uncomfortable hug, then we all sat down. I scooted into the booth first. Allison scooted next to me and Tim sat on the other side of Allison. Diana sat across from us. The conversation was uncomfortable. There was small talk of school and sports and about what kind of things Allison enjoyed doing. After about 45 minutes our visit ended with Diana asking if she could maybe watch Allison play basketball. "What?" I thought. I wasn't at all wanting to spend that time with her. As I think about it now, I really didn't want to share cheering Allison on with *her*! Tim smiled at her and said, "Maybe, sometime." I grit my teeth. We met a few other times with her, her boyfriend and their two toddler sons.

Diana and Allison talked on the phone here and there and texted each other off and on. It was hard when she started going to Allison's basketball games. I think Allison had a hard time introducing her to her coach, her teammates and their families. I really didn't want to hear Diana being introduced as Allison's *real* mom. When the time came for Allison to introduce Diana, she introduced her by saying, "This is Diana."

I have never been shy about cheering for Allison (or Nathaniel) in sports, but when Diana would call out, "That's my girl", it really broke my heart, or when she said that she could see herself in Allison. I had a battle going on in my heart. I prayed about how I could get through the emotions of having Diana in our lives. After a few games, while cheering Allison on, Diana would say, "That's 'our' girl", as she would nudge my shoulder." I still was uncomfortable about it though.

When softball season started, Diana wanted to watch those games too. Allison texted her schedule to her. She never made it to any of her games. On one particular game day, I had had a minor surgery done a couple of hours before the game started and so because I was still pretty sore, I didn't plan on going to that game. When

I went to her games, I always arrived early. This day, Allison called me when she saw that I wasn't at the school. She had forgotten about the surgery that I had earlier and asked, "Mom, where are you? Aren't you coming?" When I reminded her of why I wasn't there, she said that she really wanted me there. She said that Diana was going to be there and she didn't want her there without me being there. I let her know that I would be there. I was already in my sweats, so I grabbed my jacket and a blanket and my folding chair and very carefully made my way to the car and then the school. I was hurting, but I was there. Allison smiled at me as she sat in the dugout. I noticed her looking around to see if Diana was in the vicinity. After the first quarter of the game she came up to me and asked me if Diana had texted me that she wasn't coming. I told her she hadn't. She asked me to text her to see if she was still coming. I did. She said one of the boys had a cough so she wouldn't be there. When I told Allison this, a look of disappointment came across her face and she said, "One of the boys has a cough so she can't come. But you have surgery and you are here." I told her that it was probably too cold for the boys to come. She said that if I had a way to stay warm then she could think of a way to keep them warm too. I was sad for her, but for myself, I was, well to be honest,

I was glad. Diana didn't end up coming to any of the games. The calls, texts and visits soon stopped. I'm not sure why. Allison said that she just wanted to know who she was, she didn't want to share her life with her.

We have gotten together with Mark-Paul's fiancé, Jamie and their two small boys a few times. Allison and Mark-Paul have emailed back and forth here and there. He has told Allison that he is glad that she had a good home and has been given advantages that he couldn't have given her.

At the end of the summer of 2017, Tim and I arranged for Allison to meet Mark-Paul. We thought that we could make it a mini vacation. Because she had expressed an interest in meeting him earlier. However as the day approached she decided that she wasn't ready. I know that the day will come and she will meet him and then the curiosity will end.

After Tim and I had finally brought up what Diana had said to us about Nathaniel and Allison not being full siblings, we decided to ask them if they wanted to get a DNA test done to see if they were 100% related. They said that it wasn't important to them. Nathaniel and Allison, as well as Emily, Jamie, Mark-Paul and Tim and I didn't have any question about if Mark-Paul was the biological father to Nathaniel and Allison, we knew he was.

Allison has always been a tomboy. She has never enjoyed wearing dresses. She has never been interested in makeup or painting her nails. She has always loved sports and playing rough with her brother. When she was in 9th grade, it came to our attention that she liked a girl. I'm not going to lie, this was hard for me to take in. We opened the door for Allison to share with us if she was gay or not, she insisted that she wasn't and that the girl she was spending time with was just a friend. I believe that because she knew that we didn't agree with the gay lifestyle, she may have felt like if we knew she was, then maybe we would reject her.

Allison had had a few boyfriends during high school, but nothing serious. When we would go shopping she would want to shop in the guys area for shirts and shorts because she said that they were more comfortable and less clingy than the girl shirts and shorts and that they were easier to move around in when doing her sports. With her paper route money and tips, she paid for most of her own clothes. Allison's junior year in high school was a difficult one for all three of us. She was still recovering from her two different bouts with appendicitis and with sport induced asthma. She chose not to play any sports and spent a lot of time on the couch on her cell phone. Tim and I had a rule that if grades went below a C, then the privilege of using a cell phone would be gone and we would keep the cell phone put away until the C improved. Sometimes it was a hard battle to follow through with, but we three managed through it.

When Allison took that junior year off from sports, she spent most of her time on her cell phone, mostly on social media. I strongly believe that social media is an epidemic. It has much power to tear families, friends and people apart. I understand that there is some good in social media, like finding runaways, advertising jobs, revealing personal triumphs and new beginnings, etc. But when used the wrong way, it also has the power to destroy.

Allison had a friend that seemed to suck the life out of her. She was very negative and spoke low of Allison. You could see (and hear) the tenseness in how Allison carried herself. This once social and interactive girl of ours was becoming very quiet and at times emotional and it was hard for both Tim and I to observe.

Tim and I continued to pray that Allison would develop a healthy relationship with a guy that would sweep her up off her feet. That never happened. One day she told me (by text) that she has never been attracted to guys and that she was gay and had a girlfriend, I took it hard. She was 18. I cried. I read it to Tim, he was quiet about it. This was one of those very crucial times that I knew that I needed to 'respond and not react'. Tim and I prayed and asked God for His help with this. We knew that this news didn't stop our love for her or how much we loved her. Nothing could do that. When she came home, she seemed somewhat uneasy, like maybe she was unsure of how we were going to treat her or if we were going to ask her to leave our home. She didn't know that she didn't have anything to worry about. I looked at Allison and said, "You just confirmed what we prayed was not true. Did I plan this for you? No! Was this my hope for you? No! Do I love it, like it, embrace it??? No! But, do I love you? Yes! Do I love your quirkiness, your off the wall sense of humor? Yes! Does this change the love I have for you? No!" Then I said, "We all need to remember that one day we will all be held accountable before God on how we choose to live our lives." I drew her close to me then went on to say, "Allison, I also know that one day, I will be held accountable for how I react and/or respond to the people around me who choose to live their lives differently than I do or differently than I think they should." I gave her a hug and she hugged me back. Our love for each other and our closeness never changed.

I will be honest and say that I sat in the feeling of being a failure as a parent for a couple of days, thankfully, I didn't allow myself to live there. I had to bring my feelings to God. I had to remember that I had done the best I knew how to do in raising Nathaniel and Allison. I also had to put into practice the important *Theoddesey* tools that I had learned. It was indeed tough! I had to make myself say out loud how I was feeling and how I was going to choose to feel. I had to remind myself to not allow my past, my kids or the people around me to name who I am, but instead, choose to believe who God says that I am, He says, " (I am Blessed (Ephesians 1:3 (NIV), I am Loved (John 3:16 (NIV), I am Beautiful (Psalm 139:13-14 NIV), I am Victorious (Romans 8:37 (NIV), I am Chosen (Ephesians 1:4 (NLT), I am Valuable (Job 33:4 (NIV), I have a Purpose (Jeremiah 29:11 (NIV), I am Strong (Psalm 18:35 (ESV), I am Beloved (Jeremiah 31:3 (NIV), I am God's Masterpiece (Ephesians 2:10 (NIV), I am Free (Romans 6:6(NLT)." Something that I also realized was that I wanted to have Allison in my life. Mine and Tim's response to her would either drive her away from us and God or draw her closer to us and God. I have seen too many families allow differences to tear their relationships completely apart. I was not willing to let that happen to us.

When Nathaniel's time at the school for troubled teens was done, he was moved into a transitional house, where he could learn life tools and transition to an independent life of living on his own. He was sent to a group home in California, somewhat close to where we live. He called us a few times. He seemed to be doing well. We visited him a couple of times. He was staying in the mountains and because I have a tendency to get car sick, the two-hour trip on windy roads did a number on my stomach. We would visit with him, take him shopping and watch him and Allison either play a video game or a round or two of basketball. Watching them made my heart smile. The visits were always good.

Nathaniel made the decision to leave the transitional program after a couple of months and he moved in with a friend and his family. He took a job as a Security Guard for soccer games and concerts. He was living two hours in the opposite direction that the group home was. He lived with them for about six months and then when they moved to a higher mountain area that Nathaniel had been at before, where Isaac and his sister bought a mobile home, he went with them there. Nathaniel looked for a job, but couldn't find one.

One Saturday, Tim, Allison and I went to see him. Because the trip took about four and a half hours, we left pretty early. When we took him to lunch, we noticed that they were living in a tourist area. Nathaniel seemed surprised to see that too. I guess he was staying pretty cooped up in the mobile home. When he saw this, he said that he would look harder for a job.

Both Nathaniel and Isaac had anger issues. They let their anger fester before they would say anything to each other. At one point, they got into an altercation with each other and Nathaniel was kicked out of the mobile home. He had a couple of bags of his belongings when he called me and asked me if I could come and pick him up and drop him off in a town close to where we lived. Remember, where he was was four and a half hours away. Because I was sick, I told him that I would talk to Tim about it. Nathaniel wanted to know when I was going to call him because he needed to make sure that he was near wi-fi so he could get my call. After discussing with Tim what was going on, it was decided that in the early hours of the next morning, thankfully it would be Saturday, he and Allison would take turns at the wheel driving to where Nathaniel was. When I called Nathaniel to tell him what was decided, he was glad.

The next day, when Tim and Allison arrived where Nathaniel was, they said that he looked pretty bad. Nathaniel said that he had spent the night in a wooded area during that very cold night. Tim decided to drop off Nathaniel at a Christian Mission on the way home. When they arrived there and while Tim went in to ask if Nathaniel could stay, Allison and Nathaniel stayed in the car. Later, Allison told Tim that Nathaniel asked her why he couldn't return home. She told him that it was all about trust. We were familiar with the Christian Mission and knew that they have a reputable program, however Nathaniel didn't want to go there. Tim gave him $20.00. Nathaniel asked him if he could use it for transportation. Tim told him that he could spend it on what he needed and then he and Allison drove home. That was hard for all of us. That night, Nathaniel texted me and told me that he was cold and tired and that he felt like breaking a window of a store so he could at least sleep in jail. I urged him not to do that. That would only bring him more trouble. I encouraged him to get some sleep at the Christian Mission. When we went to bed that night, it was a restless night.

On Sunday, after church we had some church clean-up to do. While we were doing that, Nathaniel called me and told me that he decided to apologize to Isaac and that Isaac had welcomed him back. He then asked for a ride back to the mobile home park. It was after 2 pm and with the events of the weekend and work the next morning, we knew that we wouldn't be making that drive. We decided to look into getting a bus ticket for him. Tim told Nathaniel that he would meet with him in a couple of hours so they could put a plan together on getting him back to the mobile home park. We went home and while Tim called the bus station to inquire about their schedule and the cost, I put a bag of food together for Nathaniel. Tim didn't think it was needed, but it always does a mom's heart good to feed her kids, so he agreed to take it to him. They talked and made plans for Tim to pick him up early the next morning and drive him to the bus stop before he went to work. Nathaniel had decided not to stay at the Christian Mission, instead he decided to get shelter at The Salvation Army. When Tim came home, he said that Nathaniel was doing better and was glad to be going back to the mobile home park and he thanked us for our help.

On Monday at about 3 pm Nathaniel called me. He was still on the bus. He wanted me to know that he loved me and he thanked me for all of the food that I had put together for him. He went on to say, "Mom, you didn't just help me, but other people too. We had to stand in long lines before we could eat or get a bed, so I shared what I had." He also said that he met a man that had a truck and the man had orange powder all over his hands. He started talking to him and found out that he had lost his house and couldn't afford rent. He had a job at a Snack Factory, hence the orange powder on his hands, but had nowhere to sleep, so he slept at The Salvation Army after work each evening. This man's story gave Nathaniel the realization that homelessness can happen to anyone. Sadly, this man's story is the story of many. Nathaniel also told me that on the way back to the higher mountain area, he applied for some jobs and one of the jobs called him to come in the next day at 5 pm for a job interview. I told him that I would pray for him and he asked me if I could pray for him out loud right then. With a smile, I did, and I added much to my prayer while I was at it. He told me that he would call me after the interview to let me know if he got the job or not. He called me two days later and told me that he had a job as a dishwasher at a family owned restaurant near where he lived. He was ecstatic! We thanked God together in prayer. I was so excited for Nathaniel. It looked like things were changing for the better. He kept that job for a couple of months, then he took a job at a fast food restaurant. He was at the fast food restaurant for about four months when he had another falling out with Isaac and decided that he was going to move back to the area that Tim, Allison and I lived in. He told us that his job would transfer him, but that didn't happen. He moved into a mobile home park with a girl he knew and some of her family. That is where he is as I write this.

Chapter 17

CHOOSING JOY

Tim and I will soon be empty nester's. We recently learned that our son's girlfriend is expecting a child soon. We hope and pray that we will be able to play a role in our grandchild's life.

We are still and we will forever be praying for our kids, no matter what age they are. We are doing our best to stay grounded solid in our faith and strive to never be stuck in our faith. Our faith should be forever growing. I am choosing not to be the same person tomorrow that I am today. I want to learn from today so I can continue to grow more tomorrow. Life throws us many curveballs and when tough times come, it can either test our faith or strengthen our faith. I pray that you will allow yourself to begin anew and start choosing your battles more carefully so that those battles don't steal your joy.

I need to continue to remind myself to not get too ahead of myself by worrying about things that may or may not happen in the future and stay in the day I am living. Doing this allows more peace in my life and frees me to soak in the blessings around me.

I still have a fear of spiders and both small and big dark places however I have chosen to fully trust God in all aspects of my life, especially those areas. Praise God, my night terrors have pretty much stopped. It helps for me to be careful of what I watch or what I talk about before bedtime because it can have an effect on what I think about or dream about at night.

My hope to conceive may have been stolen from me, but through Christ and adoption my hope to be a mom was gifted to me. I am not a mom because I had to be a mom, I'm a mom because I chose to be a mom. My kids may not have been born from me however they were specifically chosen by God for me and in turn chosen by me. Nathaniel and Allison may not have been carried in my womb, but they are continually carried in my heart.

I know that focussing on my own problems for too long steals my joy therefore I do my best to invest in others. When I am able to do this it makes what I am going through either seem not so bad or distracts me from what I am going through for a while.

As you read my story, I pray that you were able to see God's fingerprints all over it and I pray that my story gave you hope, even if it was only a glimpse.

Remember, God doesn't always promise Christian's a trial-free life, but He does promise in Hebrews 13:5 (KJV) "to never leave us nor forsake us." I heard a sermon some time ago that Jim Jessup from William Jessup University shared about trust. He asked our congregation, while we were grieving the great loss of our Pastor as he felt that God was leading him elsewhere, if we were only willing to trust God *only if* He answers our prayers or *even if* He didn't answer our prayers? He went on to ask us if we were willing to trust God... *only if* our kids do what we ask of them or *even if* they don't do what we ask? Only if our spouse's do what we think they should do or *even if* they don't do what we think they should do? *Only if* the check that we mailed doesn't bounce or *even if* that check does bounce? *Only if* the doctor calls with good news or *even if* the doctor calls with bad news? This really made me think about God's love for us. Does God choose to love and accept us *even if* we don't do the right thing or *only if* we do the right thing? Romans 5:8 (NIV) states, "But

God demonstrates His own love toward us in this: While we were sinners, Christ died for us."

Choosing Joy is hard to do, but I am learning that it's not impossible. Choosing Joy takes effort, courage, commitment and it makes a difference. I have learned and am continuing to learn that when we are able to realize that life is better with joy than without it, it makes choosing it easier. I feel that at times, it is really difficult to look beyond the circumstances that we are in. But, I have also found that when I try to pour into others, it lifts me up emotionally. I need to daily put feet on my faith, take God's hand and do my best to follow His lead. Psalm 18:30 (NIV) "As for God, His way is perfect. The Lord's word is flawless, He shields all who take refuge in Him."

I give complete glory to God for taking the trials of my life and causing me to be completely triumphant in and through Him. I may be done with this personal story of mine, but I know that He isn't done with my life story. I have always been and I will forever be in God's Grip through this life journey that I am trusting God to lead me on. Know that you too friend, are in God's Grip!

I pray that somehow my journey has been able to encourage you, inspire you and maybe even challenge you into a deeper relationship with Christ. He is working on a story in you too. Take His hand and allow Him to walk with you on this journey that you are on. We see just what is in front of us, but He sees the big picture. Jeremiah 29:11 (NIV) "For I know the plans that I have for you", declares the Lord, "plans to prosper you and not to harm you, plans to give you hope and a future." I pray that God will give you the ability to trust Him to lead you into victory.

Always remember, **Choose Joy**!

My mom and dad on their wedding day.

My brother Donny and I. I was three and a half and he was six months old.

Mine and Tim's wedding day with Aunt Linda and
Uncle Joe.

Tim and I.

All of my Aunts and Uncles -From lower left, Aunt Tina,
Uncle Bill, Uncle Mike, Uncle Rick and Aunt Linda.

Tim and I with Nathaniel and Allison.

Nathaniel, Allison and I

P atti Robinson lives with her husband Tim in Ceres, California. They have been happily married since 1986 and have two adult children, Nathaniel and Allison who became theirs through the blessing of adoption. Ceres Christian Church has been a big part of Patti's life since 1985. Patti has been a preschool teacher since 1986 and she has a deep love for Christ and a strong desire to encourage others in their walk with Christ. She often uses the platform of Facebook to build relationships with others and to pour God's truth into the lives of those whom she communicates with.

CPSIA information can be obtained
at www.ICGtesting.com
Printed in the USA
LVHW050016061020
668044LV00012B/156